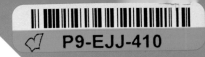

CITYPACK Paris

By Fiona Dunlop

Fodor's

Fodor's Travel Publications, Inc.
New York • Toronto • London • Sydney • Auckland

Page 1: night skyline

Page 2: La Grande Arche, La Défense

Page 5 (a): shoppers in Les Halles
Page 5 (b): café scene

Page 13 (a): old poster
Page 13 (b): Place de la Concorde, Egyptian obelisk

Page 23 (a): Eiffel Tower
Page 23 (b): Le Penseur, Rodin

Page 49 (a): posters
Page 49 (b): detail, Pont Alexandre III

Page 61 (a): stall, Marche aux Puces
Page 61 (b): Fauchon window display

Page 87 (top): TGVs

While every care has been taken to ensure the accuracy of the information in this guide, time brings change, and consequently the publisher cannot accept responsibility for errors that may occur. Prudent travelers will therefore want to call ahead to verify prices and other "perishable" information.

Published in the United States by Fodor's Travel Publications, Inc.
Published in the United Kingdom by AA Publishing

Fodor's is a trademark of Fodor's Travel Publications, Inc.

ISBN 0–679–02960–5
First Edition

Fodor's Citypack Paris

Author: Fiona Dunlop
Cartography: The Automobile Association
RV Reise- und Verkehrsverlag
Cover Design: Tigist Getachew, Fabrizio La Rocca

Special Sales
Fodor's Travel Publications are available at special discounts for bulk purchases (100 copies or more) for sales promotions or premiums. Special editions, including personalized covers, excerpts of existing guides, and corporate imprints, can be created in large quantities for special needs. For more information write to Special Marketing, Fodor's Travel Publications, 201 East 50th St., New York NY 10022.

Origination by Daylight Colour Art Pte Ltd, Singapore
Manufactured by Dai Nippon Printing Co. (Hong Kong) Ltd

10 9 8 7 6 5 4

Contents

About this book

Citypack Paris is divided into six sections to cover the six most important aspects of your visit to Paris.

1. **PARIS LIFE** *(pages 5–12)*
Your personal introduction to Paris by author Fiona Dunlop
An overview of the city today and yesterday
Facts and figures
Leading characters
The big events in Paris's history

2. **HOW TO ORGANIZE YOUR TIME** *(pages 13–22)*
Make the most of your time in Paris
Three one-day itineraries
Two suggested walks
Two evening strolls
Three excursions beyond the city

3. **PARIS'S TOP 25 SIGHTS** *(pages 23–48)*
Your concise guide to sightseeing
Fiona Dunlop's own choices, including her personal introduction to each sight
Description and history
Highlights of each attraction
Comprehensive practical information
Each sight located on the inside cover of the book

4. **PARIS'S BEST** *(pages 49–60)*
What Paris is renowned for
Museums & Galleries
Places of Worship
Cult Cafés
20th-Century Architecture
Bridges
Green Spaces
Views
Childrens' Activities
Free Attractions
Intriguing Streets

5. **PARIS: WHERE TO...** *(pages 61–86)*
The best places to stay, eat, shop, and be entertained
Three categories of hotel
Nine categories of restaurant
Eight categories of store
Six categories of entertainment venue

6. **PARIS TRAVEL FACTS** *(pages 87–94)*
Essential information for your stay

SYMBOLS
Throughout the guide a few straightforward symbols are used to denote the following categories:

- map reference on the fold-out map accompanying this book (see below)
- address
- telephone number
- opening times
- restaurant or café on premises or nearby
- nearest subway train station
- nearest overground train station
- facilities for visitors with disabilities
- admission charge
- other places of interest nearby
- tours, lectures, or special events
- ➤ indicates the page where you will find a fuller description

MAPS
All map references are to the separate fold-out map accompanying this book. For example, the Musée Rodin, in rue de Varenne, has the following information: F6 – indicating the grid square of the map in which the Musée Rodin will be found. All entries within the Top 25 Sights section are also plotted by number (not page number) on the downtown plan located on the inside front and back covers of this book.

PRICES
Where appropriate, an indication of the cost of an establishment is given by $ signs: $$$ denotes higher prices, $$ denotes average prices, while $ denotes lower charges.

PARIS *life*

A Personal View

The French state

An unmistakable characteristic of France and consequently Paris is the state's top-heavy role. Which other industrialized country allows a state bank (Crédit Lyonnais) to run up losses approaching 60 billion FF (US $11 billion) in five years? And which other nation offers amnesty to all traffic offenders when a new president is elected?

Paris remains the powerhouse of the nation, despite repeated government maneuvers for decentralization. This is where French socio-cultural trends are born, political battles are fielded, and national pride is polished. And yet it remains compact, still bordered by the *portes* (gateways) which keep the less prestigious *banlieues* (suburbs) at bay. Stay or live in central Paris and you are propelled into a maelstrom of gastronomy, fashion, cinema, literature, art ... and monuments. History is omnipresent and no ruler —whether king or president—has failed to leave his mark on the city's urban face.

Philosophy, ideas, and culture have always been favorite Parisian pursuits but at this *fin de siècle* the momentum is slowing. The population stagnates as inhabitants choose to flee big-city life for less costly environs. Live here and you spend money: the temptations are multifarious and nothing comes cheap. New buildings proliferated with President Mitterrand's *grands projets* of the 1980s; historic mansions are renovated, and state culture monopolizes every corner. Some say the city is becoming an asphyxiated museum, but spend a few days here and you cannot fail to be seduced by an enduring beauty, a grandeur, and a dynamism that few other capital cities combine.

Café life

Place St Sulpice, in the Latin Quarter

Paris still harbors a fascinating cosmopolitan character. Stroll from one *quartier* to the next and you make a minor global tour, taking in Africa, Asia, the Caribbean, and the Arab world in Pigalle or Belleville or the 13th *arrondissement* (area). Plunge into the heart of the French bourgeois soul in the 7th or 16th *arrondissements* or sweep up Parisian chic on the Left Bank. Stop at a café terrace to people-watch, read, or dream, wander along the *quais* or collapse in a park.

Explore the Right Bank and you feel the capital's commercial pulse. Follow the city's cultural history in any of its numerous museums, catch up on new films at the countless cinemas, or dive into a hot nightspot. But above all let the city lead you and do not believe the cliché that Parisians are unfriendly. Its winding streets hold surprises that even the most informative guidebook cannot cover and it is only off the tourist beat that you encounter the true Parisian spirit.

Incomparable Paris

"Paris is complete, Paris is the ceiling of humankind ... Whoever sees Paris thinks he sees the basis of all history with a sky and constellations in between. Paris is synonymous with the cosmos ... it has no limits. Paris does more than make the law, it makes fashion. Paris can be stupid if it wants, it sometimes allows itself this luxury ... It is more than great, it is immense. Why? Because it dares."

Victor Hugo, *Les Misérables*

PARIS IN FIGURES

HISTORICAL (city growth)

- 1851 Paris represented 3% of the French population
- 1921 Paris population was 3 million
- 1925 Exposition des Arts Décoratifs drew 16 million visitors
- 1940 Germans occupying Paris saw only 25% of its inhabitants
- 1954 Paris represented 15% of population
- 1954 80% of Parisian homes had no bathroom
- 1990 87% of Parisian homes had a WC

SOCIO-POLITICAL

- 10% of Parisians regularly attend mass
- 45% of Parisians go to the movies at least once a week
- An estimated 200,000–300,000 are homeless
- An estimated 150,000–400,000 are drug-addicts
- Parisians, forming 4% of the population, provide 45% of total income tax revenue
- 53% of Parisians use a car daily, 35% use public transportation
- The 1980s' per capita cultural budget for Paris was 20 times that of the provinces
- 15% of Parisians are manual workers
- 30% of Parisians are executives or intellectuals
- 20 million tourists visit Paris annually
- 45% of Parisians live alone
- The Louvre had 6.3 million visitors in 1994
- 200,000 Parisian dogs produce 11 tons of excrement daily
- 800,000 French regularly consult a psychiatrist
- 90% of French women and 50% of French men use perfume

GEOGRAPHICAL

- 2.1 million inhabitants within the city walls (decreasing)
- 10.6 million inhabitants in the Ile de France (increasing)
- 52,000 inhabitants per square mile and an average of 1.92 per residence
- During July and August over 2 million cars head south
- 40% of street trees are plane trees
- 15,000 restaurants, cafés and clubs

Paris People

JEAN-PAUL GAULTIER
Now in his early 40s, Jean-Paul Gaultier is still a prime mover in the fickle French fashion world. After formative years with *haut-couturiers* Pierre Cardin and Jean Patou, in 1979 he created his own label. From his first "James Bond" collection, through "Dadism," "Witches," and "High-Tech," Gaultier aimed to shock. Costumes for films, mobile furniture, a record, and TV shows in the UK have paralleled his two annual fashion collections.

Jean-Paul Gaultier

JOËL ROBUCHON
The man behind innovative Parisian gastronomy may be modest but his star still rises. In 1981 Robuchon took over a restaurant in the 16th *arrondissement*, and has not looked back since, accumulating gastronomy medals, writing books, playing French food ambassador, and confirming his status as France's top chef. His restaurant is consistently allocated 19.5 (out of 20) in the Gallic restaurant bible, the *Gault Millau*. Hard to beat.

ANNE SINCLAIR
An intellectual sex symbol, chic TV interviewer Anne Sinclair has become the most popular woman in France in the last decade. Steering top personalities through their analysis of the week's events in her one-hour program, *7 sur 7*, this dark-haired, blue-eyed charmer has managed to extract declarations, confessions, hopes, and fears from such key names as Mikhail Gorbachev, Prince Charles, Madonna, and François Mitterrand.

PHILIPPE STARCK
Tripod orange-squeezers, chairs with pointed legs, a laughing TV ... these are the hallmarks of Starck's design success. A "Made in France" phenomenon of the 1980s, Starck—gregarious, corpulent, and bearded—has presence in the 1990s. Still going strong is his redesign of the nightclub Les Bains Douches, while his latest gimmick is a mail-order house-kit composed of plans, a videotape, and a hammer.

Jacques Chirac
For over 18 years Jacques Chirac, the ebullient Mayor of Paris and leader of the Gaullist party (RPR), surveyed the city from his palatial working residence overlooking the Seine, the Hôtel de Ville. With a taste for reading Chinese poetry (in French) , he transformed the city's infrastructure and repeatedly clashed with the ruling Socialists until in May 1995, after two previously unsuccessful shots, he was finally elected President of France.

A Chronology

c. 200 BC	Celtic tribe of Parisii settles on Ile de la Cité
c. AD 100	Growth of Gallo-Roman city of Lutetia
451	Ste. Geneviève saves Paris from Attila the Hun
1100s	Tragic love story of Abelard and Héloise
1163	Building starts on Notre-Dame
1215	University of Paris is founded
1358	Royal family installed in Marais and Louvre
1337–1453	Hundred Years War between France and England
1430	Henry VI of England crowned King of France in Notre-Dame
1437	Charles VII regains control of Paris
1572	St. Bartholomew's Massacre ignites Wars of Religion
1600s	Paris reorganized and rebuilt, Le Marais developed
1648–1652	Civil uprising of La Fronde
1672	Louis XIV moves to Versailles
1700s	Development of Faubourg Saint-Germain
1789	Storming of the Bastille, declaration of Rights of Man
1792	Monarchy abolished, proclamation of the Republic
1793–1794	Reign of Terror, Louis XVI beheaded, inauguration of the Musée du Louvre
1804	Napoleon Bonaparte crowned Emperor
1800–1814	Building of imperial monuments. Founding of

	Grandes Ecoles, increased centralization
1830	Bourbons overthrown, Louis-Philippe crowned
1848	Revolution topples Louis-Philippe; Second Republic headed by Napoléon III
1852–1870	Baron Haussmann transforms urban Paris
1870–1871	Paris besieged by Prussians, civil uprising of the Commune, Republic restored
1889	Eiffel Tower built for Exposition Universelle
1900	Grand and Petit Palais built for Exposition Universelle; first métro line opens
c. 1908	Modernism is born in Montmartre with Picasso
1914–1918	Paris bombarded by German cannon, Big Bertha
1925	Exposition des Arts Décoratifs introduces Art Deco style
1940	Nazis occupy Paris
1944	Liberation of Paris led by Général de Gaulle
1954	National funeral for writer Colette
1958	De Gaulle called in to head Fifth Republic
1967	Les Halles market transferred to Rungis
1969	President Georges Pompidou elected
1974	President Valéry Giscard d'Estaing elected
1977	Jacques Chirac elected first Mayor of Paris since 1871; Centre Georges Pompidou opens
1981	Election of President Mitterrand initiates *Grands Travaux*
1989	Bicentennial celebrations of the Revolution
1990	Death of iconoclastic singer Serge Gainsbourg
1995	Election of President Chirac

People & Events from History

Napoleon Bonaparte (1769–1821)

REVOLUTION

The Revolution of 1789 signaled the end of absolute royal power and the rise of popular democracy. The royal family was forced from Versailles to the Tuileries palace, but in 1792 this in turn was attacked and Louis XVI and Marie-Antoinette were imprisoned and sent to the guillotine. The year 1792–1793 marked the high point of the Terror, which was led by Robespierre, himself guillotined in 1794.

NAPOLEON

Napoleon Bonaparte's meteoric rise and fall from power (1800–1814) left an indelible mark on the capital. Ambitious reforms included the construction of neoclassical buildings, while his military campaigns made Paris capital of the greatest European empire since Charlemagne. More important was the increased concentration of the nation's culture and government in Paris, something that decentralization has still not eradicated two centuries later.

OCCUPATION

The scars left by France's Vichy régime were most apparent in Paris, occupied by the Nazis from 1940. Luxury hotels and public buildings were requisitioned, and Communists and Jews were deported in the thousands. After the Allies disembarked in Normandy in June 1944, a week-long insurrection by Parisians opened their path into the capital. General Von Cholitz capitulated after disobeying Hitler's orders to blow up the city and Paris was reborn.

"LE GENERAL"

De Gaulle's role as one of France's major 20th-century figures started during the Occupation, when he headed the Free French Forces from London, continued with the Liberation, and was consolidated when he was called from retirement to solve the divisive Algerian War and head the Fifth Republic in 1958. His rule heralded increased presidential powers, a burgeoning consumer society, and the prominence of France within the European Union.

Henri IV

Authoritarian, ccomplex and charismatic, Henri IV (1553–1610) was also Paris's first urban designer. In 1594, after renouncing Protestantism and uttering the legendary words 'Paris is well worth a mass', he triumphantly entered the city as a long-needed unifying force. His reign saw the growth of new industries, a fashion for châteaux, and the downfall of the peasant classes. Meanwhile, he instigated the building of Place Royale (Place des Vosges), Place Dauphine, the Pont Neuf, the rise of Le Marais, and the planting of 20,000 trees in the Tuileries before losing his life to an assassin's knife.

PARIS
how to organize your time

ITINERARIES

One of the pleasures of Paris is its compact scale and efficient public transportation. Visiting monuments in the central *arrondissements* is easiest and most scenic on foot and always includes obligatory café stops, but do not hesitate to dive into the métro for a short trip to more distant sights.

Moving between the monuments on Sundays and public holidays from mid-April to late-September is facilitated by Balabus, a public bus service that starts at the Gare de Lyon and stops at Saint-Michel, Musée d'Orsay, Louvre, Concorde, Champs-Elysées, Charles-de-Gaulle-Etoile, Porte Maillot, and Neuilly. The service runs between 12:30PM and 8PM and the whole trip takes 50 minutes. You can get off to visit a sight near a Balabus stop, then catch the next bus onward.

An alternative way of traveling round Paris between April and September is by a public riverboat christened "Batobus." Fares are paid either per stage or for the entire ride, which starts at the Port de la Bourdonnais by the Eiffel Tower and continues to the Musée d'Orsay, the Pont des Arts (Louvre), Notre-Dame, Hôtel-de-Ville (Centre Georges Pompidou), then returns along the same route.

ITINERARY ONE	LATIN QUARTER
Morning	Climb the tower of Notre-Dame for a bird's-eye view. Walk beside the river to the Sainte-Chapelle (➤ 39). Cross to Boulevard Saint-Michel and walk up to the Musée de Cluny (➤ 38). Continue up Boulevard St-Michel to the Jardin du Luxembourg (➤ 37).
Lunch	Relax in the gardens and have lunch in a café near the Panthéon.
Afternoon	Walk over to Eglise St-Etienne-du-Mont (➤ 52). Explore the winding streets that lead to the rue Monge. Have a look at the Roman Arènes de Lutèce (➤ 59).
Drink	Walk south toward the Mosquée (➤ 52) and indulge in a mint tea.
	Cross over to the Jardin des Plantes and the Musée d'Histoire Naturelle (➤ 51).

ITINERARY TWO — STATELY PARIS

Breakfast At the Samaritaine (➤ 57).

Morning Cross Pont Neuf (➤ 55) to the island and take a boat trip along the Seine which returns here. Wander along the *quai* at river level to the Musée d'Orsay (➤ 31).

Lunch Have lunch at the Musée d'Orsay or, alternatively, walk up the rue de Bellechasse, across Boulevard St-Germain, then along to the Musée Rodin (➤ 29) where the rose garden café beckons.

Afternoon Continue to Les Invalides (➤ 28).
Visit the Eglise du Dôme (➤ 28).
Walk along the esplanade to cross the ornate Pont Alexandre III (➤ 55).
Visit the Petit Palais (➤ 27).
Explore the Champs-Elysées (➤ 27).
Catch bus No. 42 down the Avenue Montaigne to the Eiffel Tower (➤ 26). Try and time it for sunset.

ITINERARY THREE — GREEN PARIS

Morning Start the day at the Musée Marmottan (➤ 24) then take the métro to Franklin-D-Roosevelt.
Walk down the shady paths of the Champs-Elysées to the Place de la Concorde (➤ 30).
Cross to the Orangerie (➤ 30).
Walk through the Tuileries (➤ 56), stopping for a drink at a kiosk.

Lunch Have lunch at the Café Marly (➤ 53) or in the Louvre's underground labyrinth.

Afternoon Visit a section of the Louvre's immense collection (➤ 35) then recover in the gardens of the Palais-Royal.
Take bus No. 67 from the rue du Louvre to Pigalle, where you can catch the Monmartrobus which spirits you to the top of Montmartre hill.
Watch sunset over Paris from Sacré Coeur (➤ 33).

Evening Dine near the lively Place des Abbesses.

WALKS

THE SIGHTS

- Porte de Clisson
- Les Enfants Rouges
- Cathédrale Ste-Croix-de-Paris
- Musée Picasso (➤51)
- Hôtel de Chatillon
- Musée Carnavalet (➤46)
- Place des Vosges (➤47)

INFORMATION

Distance 2 miles
Time 1–2 hours
Start point Plateau Beaubourg
H5/6
Rambuteau, Hôtel-de-Ville
End point Place des Vosges
J6
Café Beaubourg, rue St Martin; Ma Bourgogne, Place des Vosges

Mére et enfant, *Picasso*

LE MARAIS TO THE PLACE DES VOSGES

After breakfast at the Café Beaubourg walk behind the Centre Georges Pompidou to turn right onto the rue Rambuteau, a colorful food-shopping street. Turn left up the rue des Archives with the magnificent turreted Porte de Clisson (1375) rising from the Hôtel de Soubise (1709) on your right. Continue past a monumental fountain (1624) on your left and the Hôtel Guénégaud (1650, which houses the Musée de la Chasse) diametrically opposite. Keep walking straight on to the rue de Bretagne where you can rest in the leafy Square du Temple, or investigate the leather-clothes market in the Carreau du Temple. Have a coffee nearby.

Along the rue de Bretagne, enter the picturesque food and flower market of Les Enfants Rouges (dating from the 1620s) then exit on to the rue Charlot. Walk down here, past the impressive Cathédrale Ste-Croix-de-Paris, a former 17th-century convent, to the rue des Quatre-Fils. Turn left, past a new building which houses the National Archives and continue to the rue Vieille-du-Temple. Circle round the garden of the Hôtel Salé, now home to the Musée Picasso, then continue to the Parc Royal, a small garden which is overlooked by a row of superbly restored 17th-century mansions. Take a look at the courtyard of the Hôtel de Chatillon at 13 rue Payenne, then continue to rue de Sévigné. Pass or be tempted by the fashion offerings of Romeo Gigli at No. 46, admire the two mansions of the Musée Carnavalet, then turn left onto the rue des Francs-Bourgeois. Carry straight on to the Place des Vosges and stop to have lunch at Ma Bourgogne.

WALKS

PLACE DES VOSGES TO THE LATIN QUARTER

Walk through a passageway at No. 9 Place des Vosges to the courtyard of the Hôtel de Sully. Exit on the rue St-Antoine, turn right and right again onto the rue de Turenne, then left to the charming Place du Marché Ste-Catherine, good for a coffee-break at a café on a sunny day. Return to the main road and cross to rue Saint-Paul, lined with antique shops. Further down on the right enter the Village Saint-Paul, a discreetly hidden bric-a-brac market, then emerge on the other side into the rue des Jardins Saint-Paul. Here you see the largest remaining section of Philippe-Auguste's city wall. Turn left, then right along the rue de l'Ave Maria to reach the Hôtel de Sens, an exceptional example of 15th-century Gothic architecture. Look at the courtyard and the small formal garden behind the mansion. From here cross the Pont Marie to the Ile Saint-Louis. End your day in the web of Latin Quarter streets across the Seine.

THE SIGHTS

- Place des Vosges
- Village Saint-Paul (➤77)
- Philippe-Auguste's city wall
- Hôtel de Sens
- Ile Saint-Louis (➤44)

INFORMATION

Distance approximately 1 mile
Time 1–2 hours
Start point Place des Vosges
J6
Bastille, Chemin-Vert, St-Paul
End point Latin Quarter, around Boulevard St-Michel, Rue St-Jacques
G6/7, H6/7

Place des Vosges

Evening Strolls

INFORMATION

Start point Place du Châtelet
End point Ile de la Cité
H6
Châtelet

INFORMATION

Start point Place de la Bastille
End point Place des Vosges
JK6
Bastille

THE SEINE

Start at Châtelet and walk toward the Louvre along the embankment opposite the illuminated Conciergerie, the Monnaie (Mint), and the Institut de France. At the Louvre make a detour into the Cour Carrée, magnificently lit and often deserted at night. Return to the river, cross the lively Pont des Arts, then walk back along the opposite bank, this time with views north of the stately Samaritaine and the Palais de Justice on the Ile de la Cité. Continue toward St-Michel, then cross over to Notre-Dame and make your way around the north side of the island, which offers views of the Ile Saint-Louis, the Hôtel de Ville and the Gothic Tour Saint-Jacques towering over the Place du Châtelet.

BASTILLE

From the Place de la Bastille walk up the rue de la Roquette until the road forks. Turn right along the bustling pedestrian street of rue de Lappe, which is packed with bars, nightclubs, and restaurants, (keep an eye out for No. 71, a fine 18th-century house). Then turn left into the rue de Charonne. Pass art galleries and more bars before cutting back to the rue de la Roquette via the rue Keller. Notre-Dame de l'Espérance looms on your right and at No. 68 there is a fountain (1839). Back at the fork turn right along rue Daval and cross two boulevards to rue du Pas de la Mule which leads to the Place des Vosges.

Notre-Dame

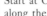

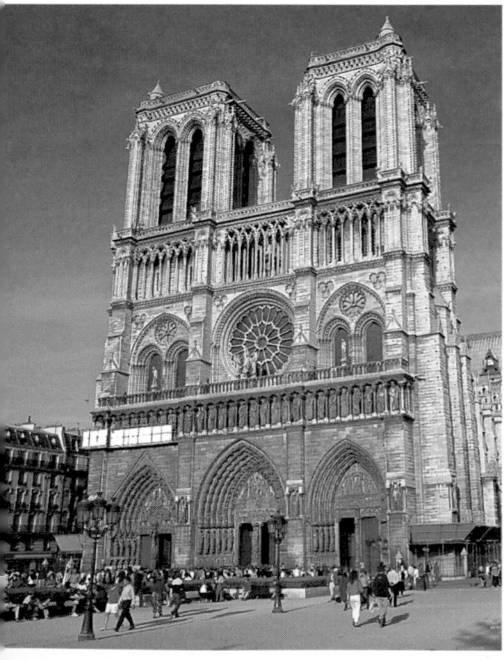

Organized Sightseeing

WALKING TOURS

CAISSE DES MONUMENTS HISTORIQUES ET DES SITES

Daily program of walking tours with lecturers.
62 rue Saint-Antoine, 75004 44 61 21 69 Bastille, Saint-Paul Moderate.

The **Ville de Paris** (municipality) offers guided tours to the Parc de Bagatelle, the Parc André Citroën, and the Père Lachaise, Montmartre, and Passy cemeteries.
40 67 97 00 (walks) 40 71 76 47 (recorded information).

BOAT TRIPS

BATEAUX PARISIENS TOUR EIFFEL

Rive Gauche, port de la Bourdonnais 44 11 33 44 Mon–Thu, 10–6; Fri–Sun, 10–9 Trocadéro Very expensive

BATEAUX VEDETTES DU PONT-NEUF

Classic one-hour trip along the Seine.
Square du Vert Galant, 75001 47 05 71 29 Daily, 10–7 Pont-Neuf Expensive

CANAUXRAMA

Three-hour canal trip (part underground) between the Bastille and the Bassin de la Villette. Booking essential.
Bassin de la Villette, 13 Quai de la Loire, 75019 42 39 15 00 Departures at 9:30 and 2:45 from Bassin de la Villette, 9:45 and 2:30 from the Port de l'Arsenal, Bastille Jaurès or Bastille Very expensive

BICYCLE TOURS

PARIS BIKE

Tours of Paris and further afield on mountain bikes (VTT).
83 rue Daguerre, 75013 43 20 67 60 3-hour circuits and weekend trips Denfert-Rochereau Expensive

PARIS À VÉLO

9 rue Jacques Coeur, 75004 48 87 60 01 Short and long trips Bastille Expensive

Paris's canals

Cruising Paris's canals offers a more idiosyncratic view of Paris than the usual Seine trip. The revamped Arsenal dock at the Bastille (1806) is the kickoff for an underground vaulted passage which reemerges at the Canal Saint-Martin. Chestnut trees, swing bridges, locks, the Hôtel du Nord (of celluloid fame), and modern apartment blocks lead to the Bassin de la Villette with its famous Rotonde (built by Ledoux in 1789). From here the Canal de l'Ourcq continues to the Parc de la Villette and then on eastwards for a further 67miles.

EXCURSIONS

INFORMATION

Versailles

- Château de Versailles
- 30 84 74 00
- State Apartments: Tue–Sun, May–Sep 9–6, Oct–Apr 9–5; Grand and Petit Trianon: Tue–Sun, May–Sep 10–6, Oct–Apr 10–5; Park: daily 7AM–sunset
- Cafés, restaurants
- RER Line C Versailles Rive-Gauche
- Few
- Château: expensive; park: free
- Fountains operate May–Sep, Sun 3:30–5; guided tours

Vaux-le-Vicomte

- Château de Vaux-le-Vicomte, 77950 Maincy
- 64 14 41 90
- Daily, Apr–Oct, 10–6; Nov–Mar, 11–5
- Restaurant
- SNCF Gare de Lyon to Melun, then taxi
- Few
- Expensive
- Guided tours; fountains operate second and last Sat of month, May–Oct, 3–6; Candlelit tours May–Sep, Sat 8:30PM–11PM

Giverny

- Fondation Claude Monet, 27620 Giverny
- 32 51 28 21
- Apr–Oct, Tue–Sun 10–6
- Restaurant
- SNCF Gare St-Lazare to Vernon, then bus, rent a bike or walk (3.5 miles)
- Good
- Expensive

CHÂTEAU AND PARK OF VERSAILLES

Few people miss visiting Versailles, the ultimate symbol of French grandeur and sophistication, and the backdrop to the death throes of the monarchy. In 1661, when Louis XIV announced his intention of moving his court to this deserted swamp, it was to create a royal residence, seat of government, and home to French nobility. Building continued until his death in 1715 by which time the 250-acre park had been tamed to perfection by Le Nôtre. Hundreds of statues, follies, and fountains, and the royal love nests of the Grand and Petit Trianon relieve the formal symmetry while rowboats, bicycles, and a minitrain now offer instant relief from history. Inside the château, visit the Grands Appartements (the official court and entertainment halls) which include the staggeringly ornate Hall of Mirrors with painted ceilings by Lebrun. The Petits Appartements (the royal living quarters) display France's most priceless examples of 18th-century decoration and may be visited by guided tour only.

The Latona fountain, Versailles

VAUX-LE-VICOMTE

About 30 miles southeast of Paris lies the inspiration for Versailles, a château erected in 1656 by Louis XIV's ambitious Regent and Minister of Finance, Nicolas Fouquet, who employed France's most talented artists and craftsmen. Five years later a château-warming party of

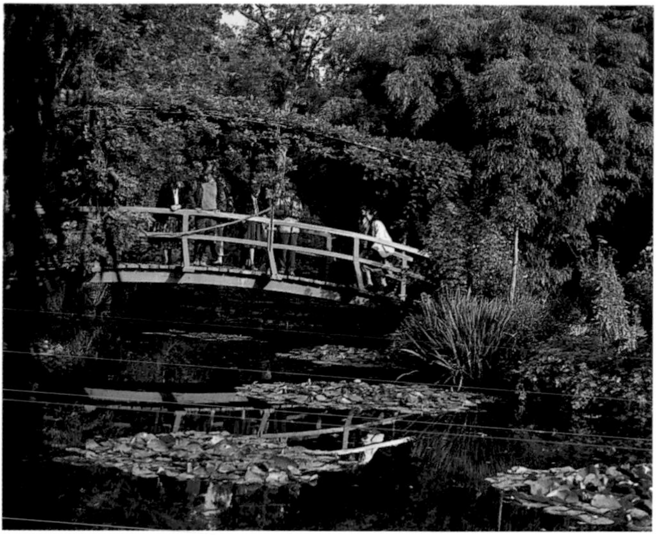

The lily pond at Giverny

extravagant proportions provoked Louis XIV's envy and Fouquet's subsequent arrest and imprisonment for embezzlement. Today the interior and magnificent grounds have been entirely restored and include the Musée des Equipages (horse-drawn carriages) in the stables. Inside the château, resplendent with Lebrun's painted ceilings, do not miss the rich Chambre du Roi. In front of the château's neoclassical façade stretch terraces and lawns, fountains, and statues ending at a canal. If you have time, continue your stroll in the woods beyond.

GIVERNY

This small Normandy village is famous for one reason—Claude Monet. Monet lived in the village from 1883 until his death in 1926, inspiring a local artists' colony and producing some of Impressionism's most famous and startling canvases. His carefully tended garden with its Japanese-style lily pond gradually became his sole inspiration, and was as important to him as his painting. Only reproductions of his works are displayed here but the colorfully painted house, his personal collection of Japanese prints, and the beautiful garden together offer a wonderful day out. May/June, when the borders are a riot of color, is the best time for the flowers.

Le Petit Trianon

The Petit Trianon, the jewel in the crown of French neoclassical architecture, was built for Louis XV's mistress, Madame du Barry, and later presented by Louis XVI to his wife, Marie-Antoinette (who was to utter the inept words "let them eat cake" from her royal chambers as the angry mob clamored for bread below). In a pursuit of the simple life, she transformed the grounds into a "wild" park complete with a make-believe village where she tended sheep.

What's On

Information on current events is best found in **Pariscope**, an inexpensive weekly listings magazine (out on Wednesday) which covers everything from concerts to cinema, theater, sports, nightclubs; it has a useful section in English. **Figaroscope** comes with *Le Figaro* on Wednesdays and also offers a good round-up of current events.

JANUARY	America Stakes at Vincennes racecourse.
FEBRUARY	National Rugby Tournament.
MARCH	International Jumping at Palais Omnisports de Paris Bercy.
APRIL	International Paris fair with stands promoting gastronomy, tourism, and publications from all over the world.
MAY	May 1, Labor Day, sees endless processions, thousands of bouquets of symbolic lily-of-the-valley, and no newspapers. The end of World War II is celebrated on May 8.
JUNE	Crowds spring to life on Midsummer's Night for the *Fête de la Musique*—a government-sponsored event which schedules major rock or world-music bands. The *Course des Garçons de Café* in late June: over 500 waiters and waitresses career along the streets, each armed with tray, bottle, and glasses.
JULY	Number one on the French festival calendar is Bastille Day (**July 14**), which celebrates the 1789 storming of the Bastille. Fireworks and street dances boom out on the evening of July13 while the 14th itself is devoted to a military parade on the Champs-Elysées.
AUGUST	Annual exodus or *Fête des villages*: outdoor concerts and street theater in each quartier.
SEPTEMBER	*Fête à Neu-Neu*, a fair in the Bois de Boulogne. From mid-September until the end of December, music, theater, and dance performances throughout the city in the *Festival d'Automne à Paris*.
OCTOBER	*Foire International d'Art Contemporain*, Paris's biggest modern art fair, at the Grand Palais.
NOVEMBER	Liberal amounts of wine descend on the third Thursday in November when the first bottles of *Beaujolais Nouveau* hit Paris. Antiques fair at Pelouse d'Auteuil, place de la porte de Passy.
DECEMBER	Paris International Boat Show at the Porte de Versailles.

PARIS's top 25 sights

The sights are numbered from west to east across the city

1

Musée Marmottan

HIGHLIGHTS

- *Impression—soleil levant,* Monet
- *Bouquet de Fleurs,* Gauguin
- Gold table-tray
- Geographical clock
- *Promenade près d'Argenteuil,* Monet
- *Charing Cross Bridge,* Monet
- *L'Allée des Rosiers,* Monet
- *Le Pont Japonais,* Monet
- Monet's water lilies series
- Monet's spectacles

INFORMATION

- B6
- 2 rue Louis-Boilly 75016
- 42 24 07 02
- Tue–Sun 10–5:30
- La Muette
- 32
- RER Line C Boulainvilliers
- Expensive
- Bois de Boulogne (➤56)

One of the few incentives to get me out into the residential 16th arrondissement is the Marmottan, where a mesmerizing collection of Monet paintings makes a welcome escape from the often colorless Parisian landscape.

Rich donations This often overlooked treasure of Parisian culture offers an eclectic collection built up over the years from the original donation of Renaissance and First Empire paintings and furniture given to the nation by the art historian Paul Marmottan in 1932. His discreetly elegant 19th-century mansion, furnished with Renaissance tapestries and sculptures and Napoleonic furniture, was later given an extra boost by an exceptional donation from Michel Monet of 65 works by his father, Claude Monet the Impressionist painter, as well as by the stunning Wildenstein collection of 230 illustrated manuscripts from the 13th to 16th centuries. Works by Monet's contemporaries Gauguin, Renoir, Pissarro, Sisley, Berthe Morisot, and Gustave Caillebotte add to the Impressionist focus, but it is above all Monet's luminous canvases of dappled irises, wisteria, and water lilies, dating from his last years at Giverny, that are memorable.

Shame It happens even to the best of museums, but when nine major paintings were stolen from the Marmottan in 1985 it caused acute embarrassment, not least because the booty included Monet's seminal work, *Impression—soleil levant,* which gave the movement its name. After a police operation on a worldwide scale, the plundered paintings were discovered five years later in Corsica and are now once again on display, needless to say under greatly increased security measures.

Top: Impression—soleil levant, *Monet*

2

PALAIS DE CHAILLOT

With its majestic wings curving toward the Eiffel Tower across the Seine and its monumental presence, the Palais de Chaillot impresses, but it also has a human aspect—roller-skating heroes, mime artists, and Sunday promenaders.

Attractions The 1937 Exposition Universelle instigated the Palais de Chaillot's strict colonnaded forms punctuated with bronze statues which overlook terraces and fountains. Art Deco stops with the architecture, leaving four museums, a theater, and the Cinémathèque Française to take over inside. The west wing houses the Musée de l'Homme and the Musée de la Marine, the former catering to anthropological leanings and the latter to maritime and naval interests. A newly converted gallery at the Musée de l'Homme houses temporary thematic exhibitions, while the main collection gathers dust upstairs. On the top floor the Salon de la Musique displays some 500 "world" musical instruments used for Sunday concerts.

An exhibit in the marine museum

Illusions In the east wing nestles an extraordinary museum, the Musée des Monuments Français, conceived by the 19th-century medievalist architect, Viollet-le-Duc. Full-scale replicas and casts of French architectural features from pre-Roman times to the 19th century include gargoyles, frescoes, stained glass, statues, and even a fountain. More replicas of reality can be found in the adjoining Musée du Cinéma, which traces the evolution of filmmaking through early movie cameras, sets, models, and costumes.

HIGHLIGHTS

- Napoleon's imperial barge
- *Ports de France*, Vernet
- *Le Valmy*
- African frescoes
- Javanese gamelan orchestra
- King Béhanzin
- Reproduction of St-Savin-sur-Gartempe
- Baroque fountain
- Fritz Lang's robot
- Rudolf Valentino costume

INFORMATION

- D5
- Place du Trocadéro 75016
- 45 53 31 70 (Marine), 44 05 72 72 (Homme), 44 05 39 10 (Monuments), 45 53 74 39 (Cinéma)
- Wed–Mon, Marine, 10–6; Homme, 9:45–5:15; Monuments, 10–6; Cinéma, by guided tour only, Wed–Sun 10, 11AM, 2, 3, 4, 5PM, (phone to book).
- "Le Totem" restaurant in the west wing
- Trocadéro
- 22, 30, 32, 63
- Few
- Moderate
- Musée d'Art Moderne de la Ville de Paris, Musée Guimet (➤ 50)
- Guided tours of Marine on request; ethnological films at Homme at 2:30 Sat, Sun

3

Eiffel Tower

HIGHLIGHTS

- Panoramic views
- Bust of Eiffel

DID YOU KNOW?

- Weight: over 7,700 tons
- Made of 15,000 iron sections
- Height: 1,050 feet
- Top platform at 906 feet
- 1,652 steps to the top
- 55 tons of paint needed to repaint it
- 370 suicides

INFORMATION

- D6
- Champs de Mars 75007
- 44 11 23 45
- Daily 9:30AM–11PM; Jul–Aug, 9:30AM–midnight
- La Belle France (1st floor ☎ 45 55 20 04), Jules Verne (2nd floor ☎ 45 55 61 44)
- Bir-Hakeim
- 42, 82
- RER Line C, Tour Eiffel
- Very good (to 2nd floor)
- Very expensive, stairs cheap
- Les Invalides (➤28)

It could be a cliché but it isn't. The powerful silhouette of Eiffel's marvel of engineering is still for me a stirring sight, especially at night when its delicate, lace-like iron structure comes to the fore.

Glittering feat Built in a record two years for the 1889 Exposition Universelle, the controversial Eiffel Tower was never intended to be a permanent feature of the city. However, in 1910 it was finally saved for posterity, so preparing the way for today's 4 million annual visitors. Avoid long lines for the elevator by visiting the tower at night, when it fully lives up to its romantic image and provides a glittering spectacle—whether the 292,000-watt illumination of the "staircase to infinity" itself or the carpet of nocturnal Paris unfolding at its feet.

Violent reactions Gustave Eiffel was a master of cast-iron structures whose prolific output included hundreds of factories, churches, railroad viaducts, and bridges on four continents. His 1,050-foot tower attracted vociferous opposition, but his genius was vindicated by the fact that it sways no more than 5 inches in high winds and for 40 years remained the world's highest structure. Eiffel kept an office there until his death in 1923; from here he may have seen the Comte de Lambert, who in 1909 circled above the tower in a flying-machine, or a less fortunate Icarus who plummeted to his death from the parapet in 1912.

4

CHAMPS-ELYSÉES & ARC DE TRIOMPHE

Like me, you may not be enamoured of fast-food outlets and airline offices, both major features of this once-glamorous avenue. But a recent facelift has upgraded the tackiness, and nothing can change the magnificent east–west perspective.

Slow start It was Marie de Médicis, wife of Henri IV, who first made this a fashionable boulevard in 1616 but it was the celebrated landscape designer André Le Nôtre who contributed to its name—Elysian Fields—by planting alleys of trees and gardens. The heyday came in 1824 when new sidewalks and fountains made it the most fashionable promenading spot in Paris, with cafés and restaurants catering to a well-heeled clientèle. Crowning the cake was the Arc de Triomphe (➤57), commissioned by Napoleon, and the 1900 Exposition Universelle added the glass and iron domes of the Grand Palais (which includes the Palais de la Découverte) and the Petit Palais at the lower end.

Parades Despite being dominated by commercial and tourist facilities, the Champs-Elysées remains the symbolic focal point for national ceremonies, whether the traditional July 14 military parade, Armistice Day's wreath-laying at the Arc de Triomphe, or the fast-pedaling *grande finale* of the Tour de France. A recent highlight was the 1989 Bicentennial procession when Jessye Norman led a spectacular host of swaying performers down to the Place de la Concorde.

Luxury These days the Champs-Elysées may be dominated by car showrooms, but there are still plush cinemas, upscale stores, and one or two fashionable watering holes to tempt those who want to see and be seen.

HIGHLIGHTS

- Arc de Triomphe
- Rude's "Marseillaise" sculpture on Arc de Triomphe
- L'Etoile
- Bluebell Girls at Lido
- "Fouquets" restaurant
- Palais de l'Elysée
- "Ledoyen" restaurant
- Grand Palais
- Petit Palais
- Philatelists' market

INFORMATION

- D4
- Champs-Elysées 75008
- Grand Palais, 44 13 17 17; Petit Palais, 42 65 12 73
- Grand Palais, Wed–Mon 10–8; Petit Palais, Tue–Sun 10–5:40; Palais de la Découverte, Tue-Sat 9:30–6; Sun 10–7,
- Grand Palais: average cafeteria, cafés, and restaurants on Champs-Elysées
- Charles-de-Gaulle Etoile, Georges V, Franklin Roosevelt, Champs-Elysées-Clémenceau
- 32, 42, 73
- Good
- Moderate to expensive
- Place de la Concorde (➤30)
- Photo library and scientific films in Palais de la Découverte

5

Les Invalides

HIGHLIGHTS

- 643-foot façade
- Sword and armor of François I
- Salle Orientale
- Napoleon's stuffed horse
- *Emperor Napoleon,* Ingres
- Galerie des Plans-Reliefs
- Napoleon's tomb
- Dome
- 17th-century organ
- A Renault light tank

INFORMATION

- E6
- Esplanade des Invalides 75007
- 44 42 37 67 (Musée de l'armée)
- Daily Oct–Mar, 10– 5; Apr–Sep, 10–6
- La Tour Maubourg, Invalides, Varenne
- 28, 49, 69, 82, 92
- RER Line C Invalides
- Good
- Expensive
- Musée Rodin (➤29)
- Guided tours on request 45 51 95 05; films on World Wars I and II

The gilded dome rising above the Hôtel des Invalides reminds me of the pomp and glory of France's two greatest promoters—the Sun King, who built Les Invalides, and the power-hungry Napoleon Bonaparte, who is entombed there.

Glory The vast, imposing edifice of Les Invalides was built to house invalided soldiers, a handful of whom still live there. Its classical façade and majestic Cour d'Honneur date from the 1670s with the ornate Eglise du Dôme completed in 1706 and the long grassy esplanade established soon after. Home to military institutions, Les Invalides is also a memorial to the endless battles and campaigns that have marked French history and which are extensively illustrated in the Musée de l'Armée. Here you can trace the evolution of warfare from early days to World War II, and there are daily screenings of war films.

The Cour d'Honneur

Tombs There are more relics inside the Eglise St-Louis, where tattered enemy standards hang despondently from cornices, but it is above all the baroque cupolas, arches, columns, and sculptures of the Eglise du Dôme that highlight France's military achievements and heroes. Tombs of generals fill the chapels while the circular crypt contains Napoleon's grandiose sarcophagus (which incorporates six successive layers) guarded by 12 statues, symbols of his military campaigns.

6

MUSÉE RODIN

As a complete antidote to the military might of Les Invalides, wander into this enchanting museum, often forgotten by Parisians. This surprisingly peaceful enclave lifts you out of the hurly-burly of the boulevards into another sphere.

Hard times This rococo mansion, built for a prosperous wig-maker in 1730, has a checkered history. One owner (Maréchal de Biron) was sent to the guillotine, and the house has been used successively as a dance hall, convent, school, and as artists' studios. Rodin lived here from 1908 until his death in 1917, with neighbors such as the poet Rainer Maria Rilke and dancer Isadora Duncan. In 1919 it was transformed into a museum.

Sculpture The elegant, luminous interior houses the collection of works that Rodin left to the nation on his death in 1917. It ranges from his early academic sketches to the later watercolors and displays many of his most celebrated white marble and bronze sculptures, including *The Kiss*. There are busts of the composer Mahler, the suffragette Eva Fairfax, and Victor Hugo to name but a few, as well as a series of studies of Balzac in paunchy splendor. Alongside the Rodins are works by his contemporaries, in particular his tragic mistress and model, Camille Claudel, as well as Eugène Carrière, Munch, Renoir, Monet, and Van Gogh. Rodin's furniture and antiques complete this exceptional collection.

Retreat The private gardens are Paris's third largest and contain several major sculptures, a pond, flowering shrubs, benches for a quiet read, a converted chapel used for temporary exhibitions, and an open-air café.

HIGHLIGHTS

- *Les Bourgeois de Calais*
- *Le Penseur*
- *La Porte de l'Enfer*
- *Le Baiser*
- *La Main de Dieu*
- *Saint Jean Baptiste*
- *Adam et Eve*
- *Ugolin*
- *Le Père Tanguy,* Van Gogh
- Original staircase

INFORMATION

- F6
- 77 rue de Varenne 75007
- 47 05 01 34
- Tue--Sun, winter 9:30–4:45; summer 9:30–5:45
- Peaceful garden café
- Varenne
- 69
- Good
- Moderate
- Les Invalides (➤28)

7

PLACE DE LA CONCORDE

HIGHLIGHTS

- *Les Nymphéas*, Monet
- Jeu de Paume
- Hieroglyphs
- Hôtel Crillon
- *Chevaux de Marly*
- View up the Champs-Elysées

DID YOU KNOW?

- Obelisk weighs 250 tons
- 133 peope trampled to death here in 1770
- 1,300 heads guillotined here 1793–1795

INFORMATION

- F5
- Place de la Concorde 75008
- Jeu de Paume, 47 03 12 50; Orangerie, 42 97 48 16
- Jeu de Paume, Wed–Fri noon–7, except Tue noon–9:30; Sat–Sun 10–7; Orangerie, Wed–Mon 9:45–5:15
- Small designer café in Jeu de Paume
- Concorde
- 24, 42, 52, 72, 73, 84, 94
- Jeu de Paume: excellent; Orangerie: none
- Moderate to expensive
- Champs-Elysées (➤27); Jardin des Tuileries (➤56)

As you stand in this noisy traffic-choked square it is hard to imagine the crowds baying for the deaths of Marie-Antoinette and Louis XVI, who were both guillotined here at the height of the Terror of the French Revolution.

Chop-chop This pulsating square was initially laid out in 1775 to accommodate a statue of King Louis XV, then, under the new name of Place de la Révolution, it witnessed the mass executions of the French Revolution, and was finally renamed the Place de la Concorde in 1795 as revolutionary zeal abated. In the 19th century, Guillaume Coustou's *Chevaux de Marly* were erected at the base of the Champs-Elysées; these have been replaced by reproductions, with the originals now in the Louvre. Crowning the center of the Concorde is a 3,000-year-old Egyptian obelisk overlooking eight symbolic statues of French cities. Dodging the traffic to have a closer look is to dice with death, but plans are currently under consideration to ease the pedestrian's lot.

Grandeur To the north, bordering the rue Royale, stand the colonnaded Hôtel Crillon (on the left) and the matching Hôtel de la Marine (right), both relics from pre-Revolutionary days. The rue Royale itself, with its luxury establishments, leads to the Madeleine. The eastern side of the Concorde is dominated by two public art galleries, the Jeu de Paume (by rue de Rivoli), which displays contemporary art exhibitions, and the Orangerie (nearer the river), famous for its impressive basement panels of Monet's *Water Lilies* and rather second-rate Impressionist paintings. Visible across the bridge to the south is the Palais Bourbon, home to the French parliament, the Assemblée Nationale.

8

MUSÉE D'ORSAY

You either love or hate this conversion of a turn-of-the-century train station, but either way its art collections, covering the years 1848–1914, are a must for anyone interested in this crucial art-historical period.

Monolithic When this museum finally opened in 1986 controversy ran high: Gae Aulenti's heavy stone structures lay unhappily under Laloux's delicate iron and glass shell, built as a train terminus in 1900. But the collections redeem this *faux pas*, offering a solid overview of the momentous period from Romanticism to Fauvism. Ignore the monolithic mezzanine blocks and, after exploring the 19th-century paintings, sculptures, and decorative arts on the ground floor, take the front escalator to the upper level. Here the Pont-Aven, Impressionist, and Nabis schools are displayed along with the giants of French art—Cézanne, Monet, Renoir, Van Gogh, Degas, Sisley, and Pissaro. Don't miss the views from the outside terrace and café behind the station clock at the top.

The Church at Auvers, *Van Gogh*

To the ball The middle level is devoted to painting (Symbolism and Naturalism) and sculpture from 1870 to 1914 and includes works by Rodin, Bourdelle, and Maillol. In the spectacular ballroom hang paintings by Gérôme and Bouguereau.

HIGHLIGHTS

- *Olympia*, Manet
- *Déjeuner sur l'Herbe*, Manet
- *Orphée*, Gustave Moreau
- *La Mère*, Whistler
- *L'Angélus du soir*, Millet
- *La Cathédrale de Rouen*, Monet
- *L'Absinthe*, Degas
- *La chambre à Arles*, Van Gogh
- *Femmes de Tahiti*, Gauguin
- Chair by Charles Rennie Mackintosh

INFORMATION

- F6
- 1 rue de Bellechasse, 75007
- 40 49 48 14, 40 49 48 48
- Tue–Sun 10–5:45, except Thu 10–9:30
- Café des Hauteurs for good snacks, plush restaurant/tea room in ballroom
- Solférino
- 24, 68, 69
- RER Line C Musée d'Orsay
- Excellent
- Expensive
- Louvre (➤35)
- Audio and guided tours; pedagogical activities, concerts, and lectures

9

Opéra de Paris

HIGHLIGHTS

- Grand Escalier
- Grand Foyer
- *Apollo,* Millet
- Façade
- Lamp-bearers

DID YOU KNOW?

- Garnier's design was selected from 171 others
- Total surface of building is 118,400 square feet
- Auditorium holds 2,200 spectators
- Stage accommodates over 450 performers

INFORMATION

- G4
- Place de l'Opéra 75009
- 40 01 17 89
- Daily 10–4:30
- Bar open during shows
- Opéra
- 20, 21, 22, 27, 29, 42, 52, 53, 66, 68, 81, 95
- RER Auber
- Few, call for appointment
- Moderate
- Place de la Concorde (►30)
- Guided tours daily at 11 except Sun; exhibitions

I find it hard to take this ornate wedding cake of a building seriously, but its sumptuous and riotous details are in fact the perfect epitaph to the frenetic architectural activities of the Second Empire.

Past glory When Charles Garnier's opera house was inaugurated in 1875 it marked the end of Haussmann's ambitious urban face-lift and announced the sociocultural buildup to the Belle Epoque, with Nijinksy and Diaghilev's Ballets Russes as later highlights. Today the Salle Garnier still stages dance and opera, though many prestigious operatic performances have been switched to the Opéra Bastille. In 1994–1995 it was closed for total renovation to counter the comfort of Opéra Bastille. Rudolf Nureyev was director of the Paris Ballet here between 1983 and 1989, and this was where he first danced in the West. The brilliant dancer Patrick Dupond has steered the national ballet company fairly traditionally since 1990.

Dazzle Competing with a series of provocative lamp-bearing statues, the Palais Garnier's extravagant façade of arches, winged horses, friezes, and columns is topped by a copper-green dome and leads into a majestic foyer. This is dominated by the Grand Escalier, dripping with balconies and chandeliers, which sweeps upward to the Grand Foyer laden with gilded mirrors, marble, murals, and Murano glass. Do not miss the equally ornate auditorium, with its dazzling gold-leaf decorations and red velvet seats, or Chagall's incongruous false ceiling, painted in 1964. It is open outside rehearsals (your best bet is between 1 and 2PM). To visit enter through Riccardo Pedruzzi's library and museum, now sporting a very 1990s look, which houses operatic memorabilia.

10

SACRÉ-COEUR

Few people would admit it, but the high point of a trip up here is not the basilica but the stunning views. Do not forget, however, that Sacré-Coeur was built in honor of the 58,000 dead of the Franco-Prussian War.

Weighty Although construction started in 1875, it was not until 1914 that this white neo-Romanesque-Byzantine edifice was completed, partly due to the problems of building foundations in the quarry-riddled hill of Montmartre. Priests still work in relays to maintain the tradition of perpetual prayer for forgiveness of the horrors of war and for the massacre of some 20,000 Communards by government troops. The square bell tower was an afterthought and houses one of the world's heaviest bells, La Savoyarde, which weighs in at 21 tons. The stained-glass windows are replacements of those that were shattered by enemy bombs in 1944.

The Byzantine mosaic of Christ, in the chancel vault

Panoramas This unmistakable feature of the Paris skyline magnetizes the crowds arriving either by funicular or via the steep steps of the terraced garden. Dawn and dusk offer sparkling panoramas over the city, especially from the exterior terrace of the dome, the second highest point in Paris after the Eiffel Tower. Access is from the left-hand side of the basilica. Just to the east of Sacré-Coeur is the diminutive St-Pierre, a much reworked though charming church which is all that remains of the Benedictine Abbey of Montmartre founded in 1133.

HIGHLIGHTS

- Savoyarde bell
- View from dome
- Mosaic of Christ
- Treasure of Sacré-Coeur
- Bronze doors at St-Pierre
- Stained-glass gallery
- Statue of Christ
- Statue of Virgin Mary and Child
- The funicular

INFORMATION

- H3
- 35 rue Chevalier de la Barre 75018
- 42 51 17 02
- Basilica, daily 7AM–11:30PM; dome and crypt, daily 9–7; Oct–Mar, daily 9–6
- Abbesses
- Montmartrobus from Pigalle or Abbesses
- Few
- Cheap (Montmartre village)
- Montmartre Village (rue Lepic, Vineyard of Montmartre, Place des Abbesses)

Musée des Arts Décoratifs

HIGHLIGHTS

- Sculpted wood panels
- Reveillon wallpaper designs
- Bronze and wood cradle
- Dufour Leroy wallpaper
- Empress Joséphine's tea service
- Georges Hoentschell woodwork
- Jeanne Lanvin's apartment
- Glass radiator
- Martin Szekely *chaise longue*
- Toy collection

INFORMATION

- G5
- 107 rue de Rivoli 75001
- 42 60 32 14
- Wed–Sat 12:30–6; Sun 12 noon–6
- Palais-Royal/Musée du Louvre
- 21, 27, 39, 48, 67, 69, 72, 81
- Excellent
- Moderate
- Louvre (➤35)

Top: Jeanne Lanvin's bedroom by A.A. Rateau (1920–22)

This uncrowded museum is one of my favorites for its discreet, old-fashioned atmosphere and its idiosyncratic collections. These may not necessarily be valuable, but they offer a clear view of developments in interior design and decoration.

The collection Tucked away in the northwest wing of the Louvre, this rather oddly arranged museum houses five floors of predominantly French furniture, furnishings and *objets d'art* from the Middle Ages through rococo to the present. It was founded early this century by an association of designers to collect and exhibit "beauty in function," and certainly lives up to its role. Subsequent donations have greatly enriched the collection which, more recently, acquired the contents of the former Musée de la Publicité, thus adding graphic arts to the list. It has recently been refurbished.

What to see The collection is arranged chronologically. The ground floor is devoted to a fascinating collection of 20th-century design ranging from Le Corbusier to Nikki de St Phalle and Philippe Starck, with superb rooms devoted to art nouveau and art deco as well as temporary exhibitions. Do not miss the excellent specialist bookshop and small, designer gift-shop at the entrance. The upper floors display medieval and Renaissance pieces with better coverage of Louis XIII, Louis XIV, Louis XV, Empire, Restoration, Louis Philippe, and Second Empire furnishings, some of which are arranged in reconstructed décors. On the fourth floor a changing exhibition displays toys throughout the centuries beside an outstanding collection of dolls. Top-floor collections of wallpaper, glass, and graphic arts can be viewed only by appointment.

12

MUSÉE DU LOUVRE

Nocturnal lighting transforms the Louvre's glass pyramid into a gigantic cut diamond—just a foretaste of the treasures contained inside. It is hard to ignore the state-of-the-art renovation, but that is just the icing on the cake.

The world's largest museum Few visitors bypass this palatial museum, but definitions of personal interest need to be made beforehand, as mere wandering could become a lifetime's occupation. Since 1981 the Louvre has been undergoing a radical transformation which crowns six centuries of eventful existence and will be completed in 1997. Originally a medieval castle, it first took shape as an art gallery under François I, eager to display his Italian loot. Catherine de Médicis extended it into a palace in 1578. After escaping the excesses of the Revolutionary mob, in 1793 it became a people's museum and was later enlarged by Napoleon I, who also greatly enriched its collection.

Mona Lisa, *Leonardo da Vinci*

Art fortress The vast collection of some 30,000 exhibits is arranged on three floors of three wings: Sully (east), Richelieu (north), and Denon (south), while beneath the elegant Cour Carrée lie the keep and dungeons of the original medieval fortress. Do not miss the two spectacular skylit halls flanking the passageway from Palais-Royal which display monumental French sculptures, nor the tasteful commercial attractions in the central marble hall.

HIGHLIGHTS

- Palace of Khorsabad
- Egyptian scribe
- Glass pyramid
- *Bataille de San Romano,* Uccello
- *Mona Lisa,* Leonardo da Vinci
- *La Dentellière,* Vermeer
- *Le Radeau de la Méduse,* Géricault
- *Vénus de Milo*
- *Gabrielle d'Estrées et une des ses soeurs,* Ecole de Fontainebleau
- Cour Carrée at night

INFORMATION

- G5
- 99, rue de Rivoli 75001
- 40 20 50 50, 40 20 53 17, recorded information 40 20 51 51
- Wed–Mon 9–6; Mon and Wed 9AM–10PM
- Wide selection of restaurants and cafés
- Palais-Royal/Musée du Louvre
- 21, 27, 39, 48,67, 68, 69, 72, 75, 76, 81, 95
- Excellent
- Very expensive till 3PM, moderate after 3PM and Sun
- Musée des Arts Décoratifs (► 34); Musée d'Orsay (► 31)
- Audio and digital tours; regular lectures, films, concerts in Auditorium

13

GALERIES VIVIENNE & COLBERT

HIGHLIGHTS

- Mosaic floor
- Bronze statue
- Staircase at 13 Galerie Vivienne
- Clock
- Bookstore
- Gaultier's shop

DID YOU KNOW?

- Explorer Bougainville lived here
- Simon Bolivar lived here
- Crook-turned-cop Vidocq lived here in the 1840s

INFORMATION

- G5
- Galerie Vivienne, Galerie Colbert, 75002
- None
- Gate at 5 rue de la Banque permanently open
- A Priori Thé, Brasserie Le Grand Colbert
- Bourse, Palais-Royal/Musée du Louvre
- 29
- Good
- Free
- Jardin du Palais Royal (► 59)

The mosaic floor (top) and the bronze statue (right) in the Galeries Vivienne

One of my favorite places for people-watching and window-gazing, these connecting 19th-century passages, with their original mosaic floors and neoclassical decoration, offer a complete contrast to the fashionable buzz of neighboring streets.

Shopping arcades Between the late 18th and early 19th centuries the Right Bank included a network of 140 covered passageways—the fashionable shopping malls of the time. Today there are fewer than 30, of which the Galeries Vivienne and Colbert are perhaps the best known, strategically squeezed in between the Bibliothèque Nationale and the Place des Victoires. Bookworms and fashion-victims cross paths in this elegant, skylit setting lined with potted palms, where there is also the occasional fashion show. It is perfect for a rainy day browse.

Hive of interest The Galerie Vivienne (1823) opens on to three different streets while the parallel Galerie Colbert (1826) has its own entrances. Colbert is now an annex of the Bibliothèque Nationale, and regular exhibitions (prints, photos, theater accessories) and concerts are held in its galleries and auditorium. Galerie Vivienne is commercial in spirit, and this is where you can track down Jean-Paul Gaultier's eccentric shop, designer watches, antiquarian or rare artists' books, contemporary design, fine wines, intriguing toys, or simply sit sipping exotic tea beneath the skylight, watching the world go by.

14

JARDIN DU LUXEMBOURG

Despite the crowds, these gardens are serene in all weather and are perfect epitomes of French landscaping. Their occupants present an idealized image of an unhurried Parisian existence far from the daily truth of noise, traffic, and congestion.

Layout Radiating from the large octagonal pond in front of the Palais du Luxembourg (now the Senate) are terraces and paths and a wide tree-lined alley that leads down to the Observatory crossroads. Natural attractions include shady chestnut trees, potted orange and palm trees, lawns, and even an experimental fruit garden and orchard, while fountains, tennis courts, beehives, a puppet theater, and children's playgrounds offer other distractions. Statues of the queens of France, artists, and writers are dotted about the terraces and avenues. All year round joggers work off their *foie gras* on the circumference, and in summer sunbathers and bookworms settle into park chairs, card- and chess-playing retirees claim the shade in front of the palace, bands tune up at the bandstand near the Boulevard St-Michel entrance, and children burn off energy on swings and donkeys.

History The Palais du Luxembourg and surrounding garden were originally commissioned by Marie de Médicis, wife of Henri IV, in 1615, and designed to resemble her Florentine childhood home. The allée de l'Observatoire and the English-style garden were added in the early 19th century. A petition signed by 12,000 Parisians luckily saved the garden from Haussmann's urban ambitions, and since then its formal charms have inspired countless literary and celluloid tributes.

HIGHLIGHTS

- Médicis fountain
- Cyclops, Acis, and Galateus sculptures
- Bandstand
- Statue of Delacroix
- Orange-tree conservatory
- Experimental fruit-garden
- Beekeeping school
- Statues of queens of France

DID YOU KNOW?

- Isadora Duncan danced here
- Ernest Hemingway claimed to capture pigeons here for his supper

INFORMATION

- G7
- 15 rue de Vaugirard 75006
- Senate 42 34 20 00
- Apr–Oct, daily 7:30AM–9:30PM ; Nov–Mar, daily 8:15–5 (times may vary slightly)
- Open-air cafés, kiosk restaurant
- Luxembourg
- 21, 27, 38, 58, 82, 84, 85, 89
- RER Line B Luxembourg
- Very good
- Free
- Eglise de Saint-Sulpice (➤52)

15

MUSÉE DE CLUNY

HIGHLIGHTS

- *La Dame à la Licorne* tapestries
- Gold altar frontal
- *Pilier des nautes*
- Heads from Notre-Dame
- Visigoth votive crown
- Italian processional cross
- Statue of Adam
- Stained glass
- Averbode altarpiece
- Abbot's Chapel

INFORMATION

- H7
- 6 Place Paul-Painlevé 75006
- 43 25 62 00
- Wed–Mon 9:15–5:45
- Cluny
- 21, 27, 38, 63, 85, 86, 87, 96
- Moderate
- Sainte-Chapelle (➤39)
- Guided tours of vaults, Wed, Sat, Sun at 2PM; of collection at 3:30PM

Top: A mon Seul Désir, *one of the* La Dame à la Licorne *tapestries*

Take a deep breath outside the Cluny and prepare to enter a time warp—the days of the troubadours and courtly love recreated in its paneled rooms hung with tapestries. Here you can steep yourself in France of the Middle Ages.

Baths The late 2nd-century Gallo-Roman baths adjoining the Hôtel de Cluny are composed of three stone chambers: the Caldarium (steam bath), the Tepidarium (tepid bath), and the Frigidarium (cold bath), with ruins of the former gymnasium visible on the Boulevard St-Germain side. Important Roman stonework is exhibited in the niches while Room VIII houses 21 mutilated heads from Notre-Dame. Recent excavations have also opened up a labyrinth of Roman vaults which can be toured with a guide.

Treasures The Gothic turreted mansion was built in 1500 by the abbot Jacques d'Amboise and is one of France's finest examples of domestic architecture of this period. Some 23,000 objects compose the collection, much of which was gathered by the 19th-century medievalist and collector, Alexandre du Sommerard. Perhaps the most famous piece is the beautiful *La Dame à la Licorne* tapestry woven in the late 15th century. Six enigmatic panels depict a woman, a lion, and a unicorn, animals, flowers, and birds, all exquisitely worked. Costumes, accessories, textiles, and tapestries are of Byzantine, Coptic, or European origin while the gold and metalwork room houses some outstanding pieces of Gallic, Barbarian, Merovingian, and Visigoth artistry. Stained glass, table games, ceramics, wood carvings, illuminated manuscripts and Books of Hours, altarpieces, and religious statuary complete this exceptional and very manageable display.

16

SAINTE-CHAPELLE

Sainte-Chapelle's 246-foot spire soaring towards the heavens is in itself an extraordinary expression of faith, but inside this is surpassed by the glowing intensity of the magnificent stained-glass windows reaching up to a star-studded roof.

Masterpiece One of Paris's oldest and most significant monuments stands within the precincts of the Palais de Justice. The chapel was built by Louis IX (later canonized) to house relics he had acquired at exorbitant cost during the crusades, which included what was reputed to be the Crown of Thorns, as well as fragments of the cross and drops of Christ's blood (now kept in Notre-Dame). Pierre de Montreuil masterminded this delicate Gothic construction, bypassing the use of flying buttresses, incorporating a lower chapel for palace servants and installing 6,650 square feet of stained glass above. Completed in 1248 in record time, it served as Louis IX's private chapel with discreet access from what was then the royal palace.

Apocalypse No fewer than 1,134 biblical scenes are illustrated by the 16 windows, starting with Genesis and finishing with the Apocalypse (the central rose window). To follow the narrative chronologically read from left to right and bottom to top, row by row. The statues of apostles against the pillars are mostly copies—the damaged originals are at the Musée de Cluny.

HIGHLIGHTS

- Rose window
- Oratory
- 19th-century restoration
- Tombs of canons
- Stained glass of Christ's Passion
- Saint Louis himself in 15th window

INFORMATION

- H6
- 4 Boulevard du Palais 75001
- 43 54 30 09
- Daily, Oct–Mar, 10–4:30; Apr–Sep, 9:30–6
- Cité, St Michel
- 21, 38, 85, 96
- RER Line B, St Michel
- Moderate
- Musée National du Moyen Age, Thermes de Cluny (Musée de Cluny, ➤38)

Top: the stained-glass windows of the upper chapel.

17

THE CONCIERGERIE

HIGHLIGHTS

- Public clock
- Sculptures
- Barber's cell
- Tour Bonbec

DID YOU KNOW?

- 288 prisoners were massacred here in 1792
- 4,164 citizens were held during the Terror
- Comte d'Armagnac was assassinated here
- 22 left-wing Girondins were held in one room
- Robespierre spent only one night before his execution
- Three types of cell according to prisoners' means

INFORMATION

- H6
- 1 Quai de l'Horloge, 75001
- 43 54 30 06
- Daily, Oct–Mar 10–4:30; Apr–Sep 9:30–6
- Cité, Châtelet
- 21, 38, 85, 96
- Moderate
- Sainte-Chapelle (➤39)

The ghosts of the victims of the guillotine must surely haunt this stark and gloomy place, a prison and torture chamber for over five centuries, full of macabre mementos of its grisly past.

Gloom Rising over the Seine in menacing splendor, the turreted Conciergerie was built in 1299–1313 originally to house Philippe-le-Bel's caretaker (concierge) and palace guards, and with Sainte-Chapelle formed part of a royal complex on the Ile de la Cité. The square, corner tower displays Paris's first public clock, an ornate masterpiece constructed in 1370, although restored along with the rest of the Gothic interior in the 19th century. Access to the Conciergerie is through the Salle des Gardes, a vaulted stone chamber now plunged into shadow by the embankment outside, which in turn opens on to the vast but equally gloomy Salle des Gens d'Armes. This is thought to be Europe's oldest surviving medieval hall, and it was where the royal household ate their meals. From here a curious spiral staircase leads to the original kitchens with their four gigantic fireplaces.

Victims From 1391 until 1914 the building functioned as a prison and torture chamber, its reputation striking terror into the hearts of thousands. A network of cells, both shared and private, lines the corridor (the rue de Paris) leading to the Galerie des Prisonniers where lawyers, prisoners, and visitors once mingled. A staircase goes up to rooms relating the Conciergerie's bloody history (including a list of the guillotine's 2,278 victims); back downstairs are re-creations of Marie-Antoinette's, Danton's and Robespierre's cells, and the Chapelle des Girondins.

Top: Salle des Gens d'Armes

18

CENTRE GEORGES POMPIDOU

Late opening-hours make an exhibition visit possible between an apéritif and dinner in this still-controversial cultural center. You can take your pick between the genesis of modernism, an art film, or a performance.

High-tech culture More than a mere landmark in the extensive face-lift that Paris has undergone in the last 20 years, the high-tech Centre Pompidou (commonly known as Beaubourg) is a hive of constantly changing cultural activity. Contemporary art, architecture, design, photography, theater, cinema, and dance are all represented while the lofty structure itself offers exceptional views over central Paris. Take the transparent escalator tubes for a bird's-eye view of the piazza below where musicians, street artists, and portraitists ply their trades to the teeming crowds.

The fountain in nearby Place Igor Stravinsky

Nonstop action The Musée National d'Art Moderne, located on the fourth and fifth floors, has an exceptional collection which covers most of the 20th century. Above this, the Grande Galerie holds major exhibitions of artists or movements; the next-door cafeteria is great for views but not for food. Temporary shows of contemporary art and/or design are held downstairs in the mezzanine Galeries Nord and Sud which overlook the Forum. Don't miss the art bookshop or the photography gallery tucked beneath the mezzanine.

HIGHLIGHTS

- Design by Richard Rogers, Renzo Piano, and Gianfranco Franchini
- Stravinsky fountain
- *The Deep,* Jackson Pollock
- *Phoque,* Brancusi
- *Le magasin,* Ben
- *Bleu II,* Miro
- *Infiltration homogène,* Joseph Beuys
- Gouache cut-outs, Matisse
- *Improvisations* Kandinsky,
- Electronic countdown to year 2000

INFORMATION

- H5/6
- Rue Rambuteau 75004
- 44 78 12 33, 42 77 11 12 (information on daily events)
- Wed–Mon noon–10, except Sat–Sun 10–10
- Mediocre cafeteria with a view
- Rambuteau, Hôtel-de-Ville
- 38, 47
- RER Line A B, Châtelet-Les Halles
- Excellent
- Very expensive, free on Sun 10–2
- Musée National des Techniques (➤51)
- Guided and audio tours to Musée National d'Art Moderne; frequent lectures, concerts, parallel activities, Atelier des Enfants

19

MARCHÉ AUX PUCES DE ST OUEN

HIGHLIGHTS

- Marché Serpette—antiques, art deco, jewelery
- Marché Paul Bert—antiques, quality bric-a-brac
- Marché Jules Vallè—bric-a-brac, furniture, prints
- Marché Biron—repro furniture, *objets d'art*
- Marché Vernaison—antiques
- Marché Cambo—paintings, furniture
- Marché Malik—second-hand clothes, accessories, ethnic goods

INFORMATION

- G1
- Porte de Clignancourt
- None
- Sat–Mon 7:30–5
- Cafés and restaurants on rue des Rosiers
- Porte de Clignancourt, Porte de St-Ouen
- 56, 60, 81, 95
- Good
- Free
- Sacré-Coeur (➤ 33)
- Beware of pickpockets

My classic Sunday occupations are hardly original as they often revolve around the Paris flea markets, of which the crème de la crème is still this one. Nowhere else can you find such a fascinating cross-section of Parisian society.

Duck and banter The approach from the métro to this sprawling 75-acre market is uninspiring as it entails bypassing household goods, jeans, and shoe stands before ducking under the *périphérique* overpass and finally entering the fray. Persevere and you may discover an antique gem, a fake, or a secondhand pilot's jacket. Everything and anything is displayed here but all commerce is carried on in the true bantering style of the *faubourgs*, a habit that dates from the late 19th century when the first junkmen moved in to offer their wares for sale.

Bargain Registered dealers are divided into seven official markets, which interconnect through passageways bustling with crowds. Along the fringes are countless hopefuls who set up temporary stands with arrays of mind-boggling diversity ranging from obsolete kitchenware to old jukeboxes and cheap junk. Although unashamedly a tourist trap, there is something for everyone here, but go early—trading starts at 7:30AM. Bargaining is obligatory and prices are directly related to the weather: high on sunny, crowded days and low under cold, wet skies. Stop for lunch in one of the animated bistros along the rue des Rosiers—try the garden setting of Chez la Mère Marie at No. 82 (☎ 40 11 90 48). On weekends as many as 150,000 bargain-hunters, tourists, and dealers can cram passageways—avoid Sunday afternoons in particular, when the throng reaches claustrophobic proportions and pickpockets abound.

20

NOTRE-DAME

'Spectacular' is the word that springs to mind to describe Paris's most extraordinary monument, with its 295-foot spire and some of the world's best-known flying buttresses. One of my favorite views of it is from the quais *to the east.*

Evolution Construction started on this labor of love and faith in 1163 but it was not finished until 1345, making it transitional in style between Romanesque and Gothic. Since then the cathedral has suffered from pollution, politics, aesthetic trends, and religious change. Louis XV declared stained glass outmoded and replaced most of the rose windows with clear glass (the stained glass was later restored), Revolutionary anticlericalism toppled countless statues and the spire was amputated in 1787. Not least, Viollet-le-Duc, the fervent 19th-century medievalist architect, was let loose on a restoration and made radical alterations.

Interior grandeur The gloomy stone interior contains numerous chapels, tombs, and statues, as well as the sacristy (south side of choir) where the treasure of Notre-Dame is kept. Climb the towers—386 steps—for fantastic views and a closeup of the gargoyles. Look closely at the three asymmetrical sculpted portals on the cathedral's façade which once served as a Bible for illiterate worshippers. Then walk round the cathedral for a view of its extravagant flying buttresses.

HIGHLIGHTS

- South rose window
- Porte Rouge
- Portail du cloître
- Sculptures of St Anne
- Treasure of Notre-Dame
- "Emmanue" bell
- 1730 organ
- *Pieta,* Nicolas Coustou
- Statue of Notre-Dame de Paris
- Choir stalls

INFORMATION

- H6
- Place du Parvis Notre-Dame 75004
- 42 34 56 10, 43 29 50 40 (crypt)
- Cathedral, daily 8–7; tower and crypt, Oct–Mar, daily 10–4; Apr–Sep, 10–5:30
- Cité, St-Michel
- 24, 47
- RER Lines B and C, St-Michel
- Good
- Cathedral: free; tower and crypt: moderate
- Musée National du Moyen-Age, Thermes de Cluny (Musee de Cluny, ➤38); Ile Saint-Louis (➤44)
- Organ recitals at 5:30PM on Sun

The southern aspect of Notre-Dame, showing the South rose window (detail above)

21

ILE SAINT-LOUIS

HIGHLIGHTS

- Church
- Arch of Hôtel de Bretonvilliers
- Hôtel Lambert
- Camille Claudel's home and studio
- Square Barye
- Brasserie de l'Ile
- Pont Marie
- High-water mark, 1 Quai d'Anjou
- Helena Rubinstein's home

INFORMATION

- H/J 6/7
- Sunny terrace of La Brasserie de l'Ile
- Pont Marie, Sully-Morland
- 67, 86, 87
- Good
- Notre-Dame (➤ 43)

Floating mid-Seine is this fascinating residential island, a living museum of 17th-century architecture and also a popular tourist haunt. Join the crowds and spot an illustrious resident, but above all indulge in the island's own ice cream.

History Once a marshy swamp, the Ile Saint-Louis was transformed into an elegant residential area in the 17th century, when it was joined to the Ile de la Cité. Today, six bridges join it to the Rive Droite and the Rive Gauche but nevertheless it still maintains a spirit of its own, and residents openly boast that its food stores are unsurpassable. Cutting across it lengthwise, the rue Saint-Louis-en-l'Ile is lined with upscale groceries, arts and craft shops, and a plethora of restaurants and is also home to a church begun by Le Vau in 1664. Side streets are mainly residential.

Courtyard, Quai de Bourbon

Hashish On the northeast side, the Quai d'Anjou has a rich past. Former residents include the architect Le Vau himself (No. 3), Honoré Daumier (No. 9), Baudelaire, and Théophile Gautier who, at No. 17, animated his Club des Haschichins. Commemorative plaques to the famous pepper the façades of the island's harmonious town houses and the river-level paths offer quintessential Parisian views, romantic trysts, and summer sunbathing. Before leaving, make sure you try a Berthillon ice cream, reputedly the best in the world!

22

INSTITUT DU MONDE ARABE

It is difficult to miss this gleaming, ultra-contemporary building as you cross the Seine. Although I find it limited, the museum's collection nevertheless offers a sleekly presented introduction to the brilliance of Islamic civilisation.

Arab inspiration Clean lines, aluminum walls, and glass are the hallmarks of Jean Nouvel's design for the Arab Institute, which was inaugurated in 1980 to foster cultural exchange between Islamic countries and the West. Innovative features include high-speed transparent elevators, a system of high-tech metal screens on the south elevation which filter light entering the Institute and were inspired by the *musharabia* (carved wooden screens) on traditional Arab buildings, and an enclosed courtyard achieved by splitting the Institute in two. The Institute's facilities comprise a museum, library, exhibition halls, lecture and concert halls, and an elegant rooftop restaurant and terrace café boasting spectacular views across the Seine and pricey but delicious Lebanese hors d'oeuvres.

Museum First take the elevator to the 9th floor for sweeping views across the Ile Saint-Louis and northeastern Paris, then go down to the museum on the 7th floor. Here, finely crafted metalwork, ceramics, textiles, carpets, and calligraphy reflect the exceptional talents of Islamic civilization although the collection remains small in relation to its ambitious setting. Temporary exhibitions are often of a high quality and cover both historical and contemporary themes. There is an audiovisual center in the basement with thousands of slides, photographs, films, and sound recordings. Other research facilities include current news broadcasts from all over the Arab world.

HIGHLIGHTS

- Light screens
- Astrolabes in museum
- Statue of Amma'alay
- Head of sun god
- Rope and palm-fiber sandal
- Sultan Selim III's Koran
- Miniature of Emperor Aurengzeb
- Indian glass vase
- Egyptian child's tunic
- Hors d'oeuvres at Fakhr El Dine restaurant

INFORMATION

- J7
- 1 rue des Fossés Saint-Bernard 75005
- 40 51 38 38; restaurant 46 33 47 70
- Tue–Sun 10–6
- Gourmet Arab restaurant/tea room, convivial snack bar
- Jussieu, Cardinal Lemoine
- 24, 63, 67, 86, 87, 89
- Excellent
- Moderate
- Ile Saint-Louis (➤44); Arènes de Lutèce (➤59)
- Occasional Arab music, films, and plays

23

Musée Carnavalet

HIGHLIGHTS

- Statue of Louis XIV
- Façade sculptures on Hôtel Carnavalet
- Lebrun's ceiling painting
- *Destruction of the Bastille*, Hubert Robert
- Bastille prison keys
- Le Sueur's comic-strip
- Proust's bedroom
- Ballroom from Hôtel de Wendel
- Napoleon's picnic-case

INFORMATION

- J6
- 23 rue de Sévigné 75003
- 42 72 21 13
- Tue–Sat 10–5:40
- Saint-Paul
- 29, 96
- Excellent
- Moderate
- Place des Vosges (➤47); Musée Picasso (➤51)
- Photography exhibitions

There is no better museum than this to plunge you into the history of Paris, and its renovated mansion setting is hard to beat. Period rooms, artifacts, documents, paintings, and objets d'art combine to swing you through the city's turbulent past.

Ornamental excess Two adjoining 16th- and 17th-century town houses house this captivating collection. Entrance is through the superb courtyard of the Hôtel Carnavalet (1548), once the home of the celebrated writer Madame de Sévigné. Here attention focuses on the Roman period, the Middle Ages, the Renaissance, and the heights of decorative excess reached under Louis XIV, Louis XV, and Louis XVI. Some of the richly painted and sculpted interiors are original to the building; others, such as the wood paneling from the Hôtel Colbert de Villacerf and Brunetti's *trompe-l'oeil* staircase paintings, have been brought in.

Revolution to the present Next door, the well renovated Hôtel Le Peletier de Saint-Fargeau (1690) exhibits some remarkable objects from the Revolution—a period when anything and everything was emblazoned with slogans—and continues with Napoleon I's reign, the Restoration, the Second Empire, the Commune, and finally the Belle Epoque. Illustrious figures such as Robespierre or Madame Le Récamier come to life within their chronological context. The collection ends at the early 20th century with some remarkable reconstructions of interiors, and paintings by Utrillo, Signac, Marquet, and Foujita.

24

Place des Vosges

Paris's best-preserved square connects the quarters of the Marais and the Bastille. I always marvel at its architectural unity, and love to stroll under its arcades now animated by outdoor restaurants and window-shoppers.

Place Royale Ever since the square was inaugurated in 1612 with a spectacular fireworks display, countless luminaries have chosen to live in the red-brick houses overlooking the central garden of plane trees. Before that, the square was the site of a royal palace, the Palais des Tournelles (1407), which was later abandoned and demolished by Catherine de Médicis in 1559 when her husband Henri II died in a tournament. The arcaded façades were commissioned by the enlightened Henri IV, who incorporated two royal pavilions at the center of the north and south sides of the square and named it "Place Royale."

Celebrities After the Revolution the square was renamed Place des Vosges in honor of the first French district to pay its new taxes. The first example of planned development in the history of Paris, these 36 town houses (nine on each side and still intact after four centuries) with their steep-pitched roofs surround a formal garden laid out with gravel paths and fountains. The elegant symmetry of the houses has always attracted a string of celebrities. Princesses, official mistresses, Cardinal Richelieu, the Duc de Sully, Victor Hugo (his house is now a museum), Théophile Gautier, and more recently the late painter Francis Bacon, Beaubourg's architect Richard Rogers, and former Minister of Culture, Jack Lang, have all lived here. Upscale shops and chic art galleries, with prices to match and perfect for window-gazing, line its arcades.

HIGHLIGHTS

- Pavillon du Roi
- Statue of Louis XIII
- Hôtel de Coulanges
- No. 6, Maison Victor Hugo
- No. 21, residence of Cardinal Richelieu
- Archaeological finds at No. 18
- Door knockers
- *Trompe-l'oeil* bricks
- Auvergne sausages at Ma Bourgogne restaurant

INFORMATION

- J6
- Place des Vosges 75004
- Bastille, Chemin-Vert, St-Paul
- 29, 96
- Good
- Free
- Hôtel de Sully (➤17); Musée Carnavalet (➤46)

25

Père Lachaise Cemetery

HIGHLIGHTS

- Oscar Wilde's tomb
- Edith Piaf's tomb
- Chopin's tomb
- Marcel Proust's tomb
- Mur des Fédérés
- Delacroix's tomb
- Tomb of Victor Hugo's family
- Baron Haussmann's tomb
- Molière's tomb
- Jim Morrison's tomb

INFORMATION

- L/M 5/6
- Boulevard de Ménilmontant 75020
- 43 70 70 33
- Daily, Oct–Mar, 8–5:30; Apr–Sep, Mon–Fri 8–6, Sat 8:30–5:30/6, Sun 9–5:30/6
- Père-Lachaise
- 61, 69
- Free

If you think cemeteries are lugubrious, then I recommend a visit to Père Lachaise to change your mind. A plethora of tomb designs, shady trees, and twisting paths combine to create a peaceful setting that has become a popular park.

Pilgrimage Up in the *faubourgs* of Ménilmontant, this landscaped hillside is now a favorite haunt for rock-fans, Piaf-fans, lovers of poetry, literature, music, and history. Since its creation in 1803 this vast cemetery has seen hundreds of the famous and illustrious buried within its precincts. A walk around its labyrinthine expanse presents a microcosm of French sociocultural history. Pick up a plan at the entrance or the kiosk by the metro, then set off on this Parisian path of the holy grail to track down your heroes.

Incumbents The cemetery was created in 1803 on land once owned by Louis XIV's confessor, Father La Chaise. It was the site of the Communards' tragic last stand in 1871, when the 147 survivors of a nightlong fight met their bloody end in front of a government firing-squad and were thrown into a communal grave, now commemorated by the Mur des Fédérés in the eastern corner. A somber reminder of the victims of World War II are the memorials to those who died in the Nazi concentration camps. Paths meander past striking funerary monuments and the graves of such well-known figures as the star-crossed medieval lovers Abelard and Héloïse, painters Delacroix and Modigliani, actress Sarah Bernhardt, composers Poulenc and Bizet, and writers Balzac and Colette. Crowds of rock fans throng round Doors singer Jim Morrison's tomb, whose death in Paris in 1971 is still a mystery.

PARIS's *best*

Museums & Galleries

Other museums

If you are hooked on the intimate atmosphere of one-man museums, then head for the former home/studio of sculptor Antoine Bourdelle, recently renovated by top architect Christian de Portzamparc 18 rue Antoine Bourdelle, 75014 Falguière.
Other jewels include the Maison Victor Hugo (►47), the Musée Delacroix (►60), the Musée Hébert (►60), and the Maison de Balzac (47 rue Raynouard 75016 Passy).

Visit the Musée d'Art Moderne for modern and contemporary paintings and sculpture

See TOP 25 sights for
CENTRE POMPIDOU ►41
GALERIE DU JEU DE PAUME, ORANGERIE ►30
LOUVRE ►35
MUSÉE DE L'ARMÉE ►28
MUSÉE DES ARTS DÉCORATIFS ►34
MUSÉE CARNAVALET ►46
MUSÉE DE L'HOMME, MUSÉE DES MONUMENTS FRANÇAIS ►25
MUSÉE MARMOTTAN ►24
MUSÉE NATIONALE DU MOYEN-AGE, THERMES DE CLUNY (MUSÉE DE CLUNY) ►38
MUSÉE D'ORSAY ►31
MUSÉE RODIN ►29
PETIT PALAIS, GRAND PALAIS ►27

CITÉ DES SCIENCES ET DE L'INDUSTRIE

Vast, enthralling display covering the earth, universe, life, communications, natural resources, technology, and industry. Temporary exhibitions, planetarium, children's section and THX cinema, La Géode.
L2 30 Avenue Corentin Cariou 75019 36 68 29 30 Wed–Mon 10–6, except Sun 10–7 Cafés in park Porte de la Villette Very expensive

MUSÉE D'ART MODERNE DE LA VILLE DE PARIS

Dufy's mural *La Fée Electricité*, Matisse's *La Danse*, and a solid collection of the early moderns parallel to exhibitions of contemporary avant-garde artists.
D5 11 Avenue du Président Wilson 75016 53 67 40 00 Tue–Fri 10–5:30, Wed 10–8:30, Sat–Sun 10–7 Cafeteria Iéna, Alma-Marceau Expensive

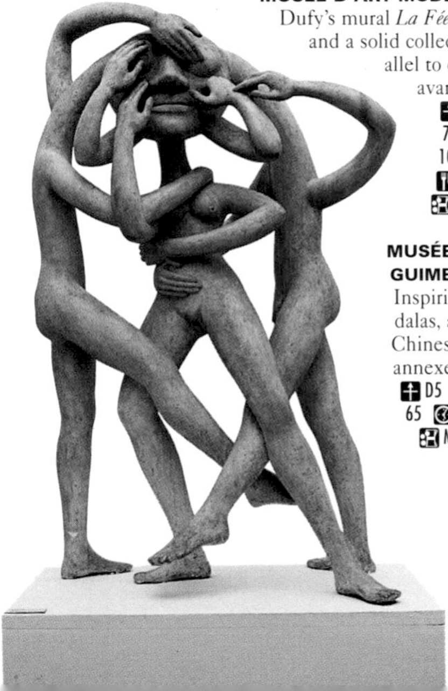

MUSÉE DES ARTS ASIATIQUES-GUIMET

Inspiring Buddhas, Hindu gods, mandalas, and Mogul miniatures. For Chinese and Japanese works see annexe at 19 Avenue d'Iéna.
D5 6 Place d'Iéna 75116 47 23 61 65 Wed–Mon 9:45–6 None Iéna Moderate

MUSÉE GUSTAVE MOREAU

A rare one-man museum dedicated to the Symbolist painter (teacher of Matisse and

Rouault) in his former home/studio. Atmospheric paintings, watercolors, and drawings.
G4 14 rue de la Rochefoucauld 75009 48 74 38 50 Wed–Mon 10–12:45/2–5:15, except Mon & Wed 11–5:15. None Trinité Moderate

Grand Nu au Fauteuil Rouge *(1929), in the Picasso Museum*

MUSÉE DES LUNETTES ET LORGNETTES DE JADIS
Eccentric display of 3,000 types of spectacles, binoculars, and monocles, including some Eskimo designs, amassed by an optician.
F5 380 rue Saint-Honoré 75001 40 20 06 98 Tue–Sat 10–12/3–6. Closed Aug None Concorde, Tuileries Moderate

MUSÉE NATIONAL DES ARTS AFRICAINS ET OCÉANIENS
Fascinating artifacts from the Pacific, Africa, and Maghreb, extending to Australian aboriginal art. Sculptures, textiles, jewelry, and masks. Kids love the aquariums and the building (1931) is stunning.
M8 293 Ave Daumesnil 75012 44 74 84 80 Wed–Mon 10–5:30; Sat–Sun 10–6 None Porte Dorée Moderate

MUSEUM NATIONAL D'HISTOIRE NATURELLE
Spectacular displays of comparative anatomy, paleontology, and mineralogy. Interesting temporary exhibitions and botanic gardens (1635).
J8 57 rue Cuvier 75005 40 79 30 00 Wed–Mon 10–5; Thu 10–10, and Entomology 1–5 None Monge, Gare d'Austeritz Expensive, reduced in morning

MUSÉE NATIONAL DES TECHNIQUES
An eccentric museum where art meets science through antique clocks, glass, vintage cars, optics, and mechanical toys. Undergoing massive renovation, some parts closed until 1996.
J5 292 rue Saint-Martin 75003 40 27 23 31 Tue–Sun 10–5:30 None Arts et Métiers, Réaumur-Sébastopol Moderate

MUSÉE PICASSO
Massive collection of Picasso's paintings, sculptures, drawings, and ceramics in a beautifully renovated 17th-century mansion. Fixtures by Diego Giacometti and some works by Picasso's contemporaries.
J6 Hôtel Salé, 5 rue de Thorigny 75003 42 71 25 21 Wed–Mon 9:30–5:30 None Chemin Vert 29 Moderate

Musée Picasso

The contents of the Musée Picasso—no fewer than 200 paintings, 158 sculptures, and 3,000 drawings—were acquired by France in lieu of inheritance tax. The process of evaluating his vast estate was no simple task as he had the annoying habit of leaving a château once the rooms were filled with his prodigious works. Eleven years of cataloguing followed by legal wrangling with his heirs finally produced this superb selection, one quarter of his collection.

Places of Worship

St-Etienne-du-Mont

St-Germain-des-Prés

The first church of St-Germain-des-Prés was erected in the 6th century in the middle of fields (*les prés*). From the 8th century the abbey was part of a Benedictine monastery but was destroyed by the Normans, after which the present church was built. The abbey was surrounded by a fortified wall and adjoined a Bishop's palace, but this eventually made way for housing in the late 17th century.

See TOP 25 sights for
SACRÉ-COEUR ➤33
SAINTE-CHAPELLE ➤39
NOTRE-DAME ➤43

EGLISE SAINT-ETIENNE-DU-MONT
Bizarre architectural combination of Gothic, Renaissance, and classical dating from 15th century. Unique carved-wood screen arching over the nave.
H7 Place Ste Genevieve 75005 Cardinal Lemoine

EGLISE DE SAINT-EUSTACHE
Renaissance in detail and decoration but medieval in general design. Frequent organ recitals.
H5 Rue Rambuteau 75001 Les Halles

EGLISE DE SAINT-GERMAIN-DES-PRÉS
Paris's oldest abbey dates from the 10th century, preserves 12th-century flying buttresses, an original tower, and choir. Regular organ recitals.
G6 Place Saint-Germain-des-Prés 75006 Saint-Germain-des-Prés

EGLISE DE SAINT-MERRI
Superb example of Flamboyant Gothic though not completed until 1612. Renaissance stained glass, murals, impressive organ loft, and Paris's oldest church bell (1331). Concerts are held regularly.
H6 78 rue Saint-Martin 75003 Hôtel-de-Ville

EGLISE DE SAINT-SÉVERIN
Rebuilt in 13th–16th centuries on site of 12th-century oratory. Impressive double ambulatory, palm-tree vaulting, and Chapelle Mansart. Some stained glass originated at Saint-Germain-des-Prés (late 14th century).
H6 1 rue des Prêtres Saint-Séverin 75005 Saint-Michel

EGLISE DE SAINT-SULPICE
Construction started in 1646 and ended 134 years later, producing asymmetrical towers and very mixed styles. Note Delacroix's murals in the first chapel on the right, France's largest organ, and statues by Bouchardon.
G7 Place Saint-Sulpice 75006 7:30–7:30 Saint-Sulpice

LA MOSQUÉE
Startling Moorish construction completed in 1926. Richly decorated interior, patio and arcaded garden. Hammam and mint-tea.
J8 Place du Puits-de-l'Ermite 75005 45 35 97 33
Guided tour 9–12/2–6. Closed Fri Tea room Monge
Inexpensive

CULT CAFÉS

Les Deux Magots, in Place St-Germain-des-Prés

LES DEUX MAGOTS
Some 25 whiskey brands, a good concentration of tourists, and the literary shades of Mallarmé, André Breton, and Hemingway. Strategic spot for street artists.
G6 6 Place St-Germain-des-Prés 75006 45 48 55 25 Daily 7:30AM–2AM St-Germain-des-Prés

CAFÉ BEAUBOURG
Opposite Beaubourg, a favorite with artists, critics, and book-reading poseurs. Discreet tables in spacious setting designed by Christian de Portzamparc. A good winter retreat.
H6 100 rue Saint-Martin 75004 48 87 89 98 Daily 8AM–2AM Hôtel-de-Ville

LA CLOSERIE DES LILAS
Hot spot of history's makers and shakers, including Lenin, Trotsky, Verlaine, and James Joyce.
G8 171 Boulevard du Montparnasse 75006 43 26 70 50 Daily 11AM–1:30AM Vavin/Raspail

CAFÉ DE FLORE
Haunted by ghosts of existentialists Sartre and De Beauvoir who held court here during the Occupation. Wildly overpriced but great people-watching.
G6 172 Boulevard St-Germain 45 48 55 26 Daily 7:45AM–1:30AM St-Germain-des-Prés

CAFÉ MARLY
The latest in fashionable watering holes. Elegance assured overlooking Louvre pyramid, and by Olivier Gagnère's intelligent decoration.
G5 Cour Napoléon, 93 rue de Rivoli 75001 49 26 06 60 Daily 8AM–2AM Palais-Royal/Musée du Louvre

CAFÉ DE LA PAIX
Excessively mid-19th century décor designed by Charles Garnier. Extravagant setting. Touristy.
G4 12 Boulevard des Capucines 75009 40 07 30 20 Daily 10AM–1AM Opéra

LA PALETTE
Firmly established Left Bank arty bar/café. Run with an iron glove by bearded Jean-François, not to be trifled with. Wonderful tree-shaded terrace in summer.
G6 43 rue de Seine 75006 43 26 84 87 Mon–Sat 8AM–2AM. Closed Aug Odéon.

The croissant

As you sit over your morning *café au lait* chewing a croissant, meditate on the origins of this quintessential French product. It was invented when Vienna was besieged by the Turks in 1683. A baker heard underground noises and informed the authorities, who found the enemy tunneling away into the city. The baker's reward was permission to produce pastries—so he created one in the form of the Islamic crescent.

20TH-CENTURY ARCHITECTURE

Grands projets

President Mitterrand was responsible for many of Paris's late-20th-century monuments. For over a decade cranes groaned as the state's *grands projets* emerged from their foundations. Intellectual criteria often came before functional considerations and consequently not all monuments operate successfully. The Louvre renovation, topped by I. M. Pei's pyramid, is a notable exception.

The Grande Arche at La Defense

See TOP 25 sights for
CENTRE GEORGES POMPIDOU ➤41
INSTITUT DU MONDE ARABE ➤45

BIBLIOTHÈQUE DE FRANCE

Mitterrand's last pet *grand projet*. Dominique Perrault's symbolic design has been dogged by technical and functional problems, so inauguration delayed until early 1997.
K8 9 Boulevard Vincent Auriol 75013 44 23 03 70 Tours of site Sun, 10–4 every half-hour None Quai de la Gare

CITÉ DE LA MUSIQUE

Finally completed in 1995 after 16 years of procrastination and political *volte faces*. Monumental design in white stone by Christian de Portzamparc houses a music school, concert hall, and museum of music.
L2 Parc de la Villette 44 84 45 00 Wed–Sun 12noon–6 Café Porte de Pantin

LA GRANDE ARCHE

A marble window on the world designed by Otto Von Spreckelsen and completed for the 1989 Bicentennial. Take the vertiginous outside elevator to the top for views along Le Nôtre's historical axis to the Louvre.
1 Parvis de La Défense 49 07 27 27 Oct–Mar, Mon–Fri 9–6; Apr–Sep, Mon–Fri 9–7, Sat–Sun 9–8 La Défense Expensive

HOUSE IN RUE VAVIN

Innovative building faced in blue-and-white ceramic with stepped balconies. Designed by Henri Sauvage in 1925 as an early attempt at a self-contained unit.
G7 26 rue Vavin 75006 Vavin

MAISON DU VERRE

Designed in art-deco style by Pierre Chareau in 1932. Astonishing use of glass.
G6 31 rue Saint-Guillaume 75006 Rue du Bac

PORTE DAUPHINE

The best remaining example (1902) of Hector Guimard's art-nouveau métro entrances with a glass canopy and writhing sculptural structures.
C4 Avenue Bugeaud 75016 Porte Dauphine

RUE MALLET-STEVENS

Tiny cul-de-sac housing major symbols of "cubist" architecture (1927) by Robert Mallet-Stevens. Stark, purist lines and volumes continue at Le Corbusier's nearby Villa La Roche (1923), now a Foundation.
B6 Rue Mallet-Stevens, off rue du Dr Blanche 75016 Jasmin

BRIDGES

PONT ALEXANDRE III
Paris's most ornate bridge, rich in gilded cupids and elaborate lamps. Built for 1900 Exposition Universelle and dedicated to new Franco-Russian alliance—foundation stone was laid by Czar Alexander III.
E5 Invalides

PONT DE L'ALMA
Originally built in 1856 to commemorate victory over Russians in Crimean War. Replaced in 1974 but the Zouave soldier remains, one of four original statues, now acting as a high-water marker.
E5 Alma-Marceau

PONT DES ARTS
The pedestrian bridge of 1804 was replaced in 1985 by an iron structure of seven steel arches crossed by resonant wooden planks. Favorite spot for impromptu parties, and street performances.
G6 Louvre

PONT DE BIR-HAKEIM
Paris's double-decker bridge, best experienced by rattling over it in métro. Built in 1903–5 with metal columns in art-nouveau style, designed by Formigé.
D6 Bir-Hakeim, Passy

PONT MARIE
Named after the Ile Saint-Louis property developer, built in 1635. Once lined with four-story houses—some later partly destroyed by floods and others demolished in 1788.
J6 Pont-Marie

PONT NEUF
Built 1578–1604, Paris's oldest bridge ironically bears the name of "new bridge." The innovative, houseless design was highly controversial at the time. In 1985 it was "wrapped" by site-artist Christo.
G/H6 Pont-Neuf

PONT ROYAL
Five classical arches join the Tuileries with the Faubourg Saint-Germain area. Built in 1689 by Gabriel to Mansart's design, once frequently used for major Parisian festivities and fireworks.
G6 Palais Royal/Musée du Louvre

36 bridges

The Paris motto 'Fluctuat nec mergitur' ('It floats but it never sinks') did not always hold true. For centuries there were only two bridges, which linked the Ile de la Cité north and south. Subsequent wooden bridges sank without trace after floods, fires, or river-craft collisions, so the construction of the stone Pont Neuf marked a real advance. The city's 36th bridge, Pont Charles-de-Gaulle, now spans the Seine between the Bibliothèque de France and Bercy.

Pont Alexandre III

GREEN SPACES

Parc Monceau

Parc de bagatelle

On the west side of the Bois de Boulogne is the Parc de Bagatelle. Its mini-château, built in 1775, was sold in 1870 to Englishman Richard Wallace, who added further pavilions and terraces. About 700 varieties of roses bloom here and its open-air restaurant offers a romantic, summer-evening setting.

Jardin des Serres d'Auteuil

Off the tourist beat, with striking late-19th-century tropical greenhouses. Terrace wall adorned with sculpted masks from Rodin's studio.

A7

3 Avenue de la Porte d'Auteuil 75016

40 71 74 00

Daily 10–5

Porte d'Auteuil

BOIS DE BOULOGNE

An area of 2,090 acres, 22 miles of paths, 150,000 trees and 300,000 bushes, and endless distractions from boating to clay-pigeon-shooting or gastronomy.
A/B 4/6 Permanently open Cafés, restaurants Porte Dauphine, Porte d'Auteuil

JARDIN DES TUILERIES

Laid out in 1564, later radically formalized by Le Nôtre. Now replanted to match adjoining Louvre. Maillol's statues rest in the shade of chestnut trees.
F/G5 Rue de Rivoli 75001 None Daily dawn–dusk Open-air cafés Tuileries Free

PARC ANDRÉ-CITROËN

A cool futurist park divided into specialist gardens, landscaped in 1980s on site of former Citroën factory.
C8 Rue Balard, rue Leblanc, 75015 40 71 76 00 Daily, Oct–Mar 9–6; Apr–Sep 9AM–10PM Balard

PARC MONCEAU

Classic park planted in 1783 by Thomas Blaikie by order of the Duc d'Orléans. Picturesque *faux* ruins, statues and Ledoux's rotunda create timeless setting.
E3 Boulevard de Courcelles 75008 42 27 08 64 Daily, Oct–Mar 7AM–8PM; Apr–Sep 7AM–10PM Monceau

PARC MONTSOURIS

A Haussmann creation designed on English models with copses and serpentine paths. Small lake with swans, waterfall, and grotto. Summer bandstand.
G10 Avenue Reille/ Boulevard Jourdan 75014 Oct–Mar, 8:30–6; Apr–Sep, 8:30AM–10PM Restaurant RER Line B Cité Universitaire Free

VIEWS

Don't forget superlative panoramas from
SACRÉ-COEUR ➤33
EIFFEL TOWER ➤26
CENTRE POMPIDOU ➤41
NOTRE-DAME ➤43
INSTITUT DU MONDE ARABE ➤45
LA GRANDE ARCHE ➤54

ARC DE TRIOMPHE
At the hub of Haussmann's web of 12 avenues, the ultimate symbol of Napoleon's military pretensions and might. Video projections.
D4 Place de l'Etoile, 75008 43 80 31 31 Daily, Oct–Mar 10–5; Apr–Sep 9:30–6, Fri until 9:30PM Charles-de-Gaulle-Etoile Expensive

LA GRANDE ROUE
Dizzy, whirling views of the Tuileries and Louvre from the Big Wheel at the heart of the fun fair.
G5 Rue de Rivoli 75001 Late Jun–late Aug, Sun–Fri noon–11:45, Sat noon–12:45AM Tuileries Moderate

LA SAMARITAINE
From 10th floor at Magasin 2, a spectacular close-up on the city's Left Bank monuments. Lunch in open air on 9th floor or alternatively dine in newly designed splendor at 5th-floor restaurant, Toupary. (40 41 29 29 Mon–Sat 8PM–1AM) H6 Rue de la Monnaie 75001 40 41 20 20 Easter–Oct, Mon–Sat 9:30–7, except Thu 9:30AM–10PM Cafeteria, restaurant Pont-Neuf Free

SQUARE DU VERT GALANT
Quintessential river-level view of bridges and Louvre, shaded by willows and stunning at sunset.
G6 Place du Pont-Neuf 75001 None Daily, Oct–Mar 9–5:30; Apr–Sep 9AM–10PM None Pont-Neuf

TOUR MONTPARNASSE
The 59th floor of this 686-foot modern tower looming over Montparnasse offers sweeping vistas of the city. Films on Paris are screened on the 56th floor.
F8 33 Avenue du Maine 75015 45 38 52 56 Daily 9:30AM–10:30PM, Apr–Sep until 11:30PM Bar, restaurant Montparnasse-Bienvenue Expensive

Pollution over Paris

The promised views over Paris do not always materialize as the capital is often hidden in haze trapped by the saucerlike shape of the Ile de France. Measures taken since the mid-1970s have helped: in one decade industrial pollution was reduced by 50% and the replacement of coal by nuclear energy and gas further cleared the air. However carbon-monoxide levels (from traffic exhaust) often exceed EU norms.

The view from Tour Montparnasse

CHILDREN'S ACTIVITIES

Le guignol

A juvenile crowd-puller going back to the early 19th century is the *guignol*, an open-air puppet show held in several Parisian parks. Shows are staged on Wednesday, weekends, and during school vacations. Find them in parks such as the Luxembourg, Montsouris, Buttes Chaumont, Champ-de-Mars, or the Jardin d'Acclimatation. Winter months see most of them moving under cover.

DISNEYLAND PARIS

Disney's mega resort struggles with financial problems but survives. Kids' paradise.
77777 Marne-la-Vallée 64 74 30 00, 60 30 60 30 (recorded information) 10–6 Cafés, restaurants RER Line A Marne-la-Vallée-Chessy Very expensive

CIRQUE ALEXIS GRÜSS

Perennial favorite with a new high-tech circus show.
F10 21 Avenue de la porte de Châtillon 75014 40 36 08 00 Shows on Wed, Sat, Sun and public holidays Porte d'Orléans Very expensive

LA GÉODE

The cinema's hemispherical screen is designed to plunge the spectators into the heart of the action with frequent showings of nature and science films Nearby is Le Cinaxe, a mobile cinema, and the children's activities at the Cité des Sciences (►50).
L2 26 Avenue Corentin Cariou 75019 36 68 29 30 Sessions Tue–Sun Cafés in park Porte de la Villette Very expensive

JARDIN D'ACCLIMATATION

Specially designed section of Bois de Boulogne with minitrain (which leaves from Porte Maillot Wed, Sat, Sun, and public holidays), playground, fairground, educational museum, "enchanted river," circus, zoo, and puppet theater.
B4 Bois de Boulogne 75016 40 67 90 82 Daily 10–6 Café Sablons Cheap

PARC ASTÉRIX

Some 22 miles north of Paris, a very Gallic theme park dedicated to comic-strip hero, Astérix. Plenty of animation, rides, games, and food.
60128 Plailly (16)44 62 34 34, (16)36 68 30 10 Apr–mid-Oct, Mon–Fri 10–6; Sat–Sun 10–10 Cafés, restaurants RER Line B, Roissy Charles-de-Gaulle Very expensive

La Géode

Free Attractions

ARÈNES DE LUTÈCE
A partly ruined Gallo-Roman amphitheater now favoured by *boules*-playing retirees. Destroyed in AD 280 but restored early this century.
H7 Rue des Arènes 75005 Daily, Oct–Mar 8–5:30; Apr–Mar 8AM–10PM None Jussieu

DROUOT RICHELIEU
Let yourself be tempted at Paris's main auction rooms. A Persian carpet, a Louis XV commode, or a bunch of cutlery may come under the hammer. Auctions start at 2PM.
G4 9 rue Drouot 75009 48 00 20 20 Tue–Sun, 11–6. Closed Jul-Aug Richelieu-Drouot

JARDIN DU PALAIS-ROYAL
Elegant 18th-century arcades surround this peaceful formal garden and palace (now the Conseil d'Etat and the Ministère de la Culture), redolent of Revolutionary history. Daniel Buren's conceptual striped columns occupy the Cour d'Honneur.
G5 Place du Palais-Royal 75001 Daily, Oct–Mar 7:30AM–8:30PM; Apr–Sep 7AM–11pm Restaurants, tea room Palais-Royal

MÉMORIAL DE LA DÉPORTATION
In the Ile de la Cité's eastern tip is a starkly designed crypt lined with 200,000 quartz pebbles to commemorate French citizens deported by the Nazis.
H6 Square de l'Ile de France 75004 Mon–Fri 8:30–5:30; Sat–Sun 9–5.30 None Cité

PALAIS DE JUSTICE
Follow in the footsteps of lawyers, judges, and crooks down echoing corridors, staircases, and courtyards and, if your French is up to it, sit in on a court case. This former royal palace took on its present function during the Revolution.
H6 Boulevard du Palais 75001 44 32 50 00 Mon–Fri 9–6 None Cité

PAVILLON DE L'ARSENAL
Well-conceived exhibitions on urban Paris and a permanent display of its architectural evolution in a strikingly designed space.
J7 21 Boulevard Morland 75004 42 76 33 97 Tue–Sat 10:30–6:30; Sun 11–7 None Sully-Morland

Bargain Paris

Nothing comes cheap in this city of light and the *franc fort.* Gastronomy, official culture, and history cost money, but browsing at the bouquinistes along the Seine, picnicking on the river banks, reading in a park, exploring back streets, or spinning hours away for the cost of a coffee on a *terrasse* are some of Paris's bargains.

The Palais Royal

INTRIGUING STREETS

Cour de Rohan

This narrow cobbled passage tucked away on the Left Bank, the Cour de Rohan connects rue St-André-des-Arts with Boulevard St-Germain and dates from 1776, though it incorporates a medieval tower. It became a hive of revolutionary activity with Marat printing pamphlets at No. 8, Danton installed at No. 20, and the anatomy professor Dr. Guillotin (conceptor of that "philanthropic beheading machine") at No. 9.

BOULEVARD DE ROCHECHOUART

Teeming with struggling immigrants. Impromptu markets, Tati (the palace of cheap clothes), or seedy sex-shops, and an all-pervading aroma of *merguez* and fries.
H3 Barbès-Rochechouart

FAUBOURG SAINT-HONORÉ

Price tags and politics cohabit in this street of luxury. See Hermès's imaginative window-dressing or salute the gendarmes in front of the Elysée Palace.
F 4/5 Madeleine

RUE DU CHERCHE-MIDI

César's sculpture on the rue de Sèvres crossroads marks out this typical Left Bank street, home to the famous Poîlane bakery (No. 8) and the Musée Hébert (No. 85). Main interest ends at the Boulevard Raspail.
G7 Saint-Sulpice

RUE JACOB

Antique and interior-decoration shops monopolize this picturesque stretch. Make a 20-pace detour to the Musée Delacroix on the delightful Place Furstemberg.
G6 St-Germain-des-Prés

RUE MONSIEUR-LE-PRINCE

An uphill stretch lined with university bookshops, antique and ethnic shops, and a sprinkling of student restaurants. Sections of the medieval city wall are embedded in Nos. 41 and 47.
G7 Odéon

RUE DES ROSIERS

Effervescent street at heart of Paris's Jewish quarter. Kosher butchers and restaurants, the old hammam, and Hebrew bookstores rub shoulders with designer boutiques. Quiets considerably on Saturdays.
J6 St-Paul

RUE VIEILLE-DU-TEMPLE

The pulse of the hip Marais, dense in bars, cafés, boutiques, and, farther north, the historic Hôtel Amelot-de-Bisseuil (No. 47), the Maison J Hérouët, the Hôtel de Rohan (No. 87), and the garden of the Musée Picasso.
J6 St-Paul

PARIS *where to...*

LUXURY HOTELS

Expect to pay over 1000FF for a single room in the luxury category.

Le Crillon

Whether you stay at the Ritz, the Crillon, the Meurice, the Bristol, or the Georges V, they all have their tales to tell, but that of the Crillon is perhaps the most momentous: This family mansion (still 100 percent French-owned by the Taittingers of champagne fame) managed to survive the Revolution despite having the guillotine on its doorstep. Mary Pickford and Douglas Fairbanks spent their honeymoon here.

LE CRILLON

An old Parisian classic which reeks glamour, history, and major investments. Suites are almost the norm here.

🕂 F5 ✉ 10 Place de la Concorde 75008 ☎ 44 71 15 00 fax 44 71 15 02 🚇 Concorde

L'HÔTEL

A Parisian legend redolent of Oscar Wilde's last days. Kitsch piano-bar/restaurant and some superbly furnished rooms.

🕂 G6 ✉ 13 rue des Beaux Arts 75006 ☎ 43 25 27 22 fax 43 25 64 81 🚇 St Germain

HÔTEL DU JEU DE PAUME

Delightful, refined small hotel carved out of a 17th-century royal tennis court. Tasteful rooms with beams and marble bathrooms, some duplex suites. No restaurant.

🕂 J7 ✉ 54 rue Saint-Louis-en-l'Ile 75004 ☎ 43 26 14 18 fax 40 46 02 76 🚇 Pont Marie

HÔTEL LUTETIA

Completely refurbished in art-deco style by Sonia Rykiel in 1989. Avoid the cheaper back rooms. Well located between St Germain and Montparnasse.

🕂 F7 ✉ 45 Boulevard Raspail 75006 ☎ 49 54 46 46 fax 49 54 46 00 🚇 Sèvres-Babylone

HÔTEL MEURICE

Classically ornate luxury, once home to Salvador Dali and before that the Nazi HQ during the Occupation. Now efficiently run by the CIGA group.

🕂 G5 ✉ 228 rue de Rivoli 75001 ☎ 44 58 10 10 fax 44 58 10 15/16 🚇 Tuileries

✳ HOTEL MONTALEMBERT

Fashionable Left-Bank hotel with garden-patio, bar, and restaurant. Chic contemporary design details, well-appointed rooms. Popular with Americans.

🕂 F6 ✉ 3 rue de Montalembert 75007 ☎ 45 48 68 11 fax 42 22 58 19 🚇 Rue du Bac

HÔTEL SAINTE BEUVE

Exclusive establishment between the heart of Montparnasse and the Luxembourg gardens. Period antiques mix happily with modern furnishings. Tasteful and imaginative extras.

🕂 G7 ✉ 9 rue Ste-Beuve 75006 ☎ 45 48 20 07 fax 45 48 67 52 🚇 Vavin

HÔTEL SAN RÉGIS

Convenient for the couturiers on Avenue Montaigne. Elaborately decorated but modestly scaled hotel, popular with American show-biz folk. Restaurant for hotel guests only.

🕂 E5 ✉ 12 rue Jean Goujon 75008 ☎ 44 95 16 16 fax 45 61 05 48 🚇 Alma-Marceau

PAVILLON DE LA REINE

Set back from historic Place des Vosges. Flowery courtyard, tasteful period decoration, and comfortable rooms.

🕂 J6 ✉ 28 Place des Vosges, 75004 ☎ 42 77 96 40 fax 42 77 63 06 🚇 Chemin Vert

MID-RANGE HOTELS

HÔTEL DE L'ABBAYE SAINT GERMAIN
Quaint, historic establishment, a former monastery. Flowery, cobbled courtyard, elegant salons, terraced duplex rooms, and friendly staff.
G7 10 rue Cassette 75006 45 44 38 11 fax 45 48 07 86 Saint-Sulpice

HÔTEL D'ANGLETERRE
Former British Embassy. Pretty garden-patio, spacious rooms where Hemingway once stayed. Bar and piano lounge. Book well ahead.
G6 44 rue Jacob 75006 42 60 34 72 fax 42 60 16 93 St-Germain

HÔTEL BERGÈRE
131-room hotel run by Best Western close to the Grands Boulevards. Reliable though anonymous service.
H4 34 rue Bergère 75009 47 70 34 34 fax 47 70 36 36 Rue Montmartre

HÔTEL DUC DE SAINT-SIMON
Rather pricey but the antique furnishings and picturesque setting just off Boulevard St-Germain justify it. Popular with diplomats. Comfortable rooms, intimate atmosphere. Needs advance booking.
F6 14 rue Saint-Simon 75007 45 48 35 66 fax 45 48 68 25 Rue du Bac

HÔTEL LENOX
Popular with design and fashion world. Chase T. S. Eliot's ghost and enjoy the restored, stylish 1930s bar. Book well ahead.
G6 9 rue de l'Université 75007 42 96 10 95 fax 42 61 52 83 Rue du Bac

RÉSIDENCE LORD BYRON
Comfortable, classy 31-room hotel just off the Champs-Elysées. Small garden and well-appointed, reasonably priced rooms.
E4 5 rue Châteaubriand 75008 43 59 89 98 fax 42 89 46 04 Georges V

HÔTEL DES MARRONIERS
Named after the chestnut trees that dominate the garden. Obsessively vegetal/floral-based decoration. Oak-beamed rooms, vaulted cellars converted to lounges. Book well ahead
G6 21 rue Jacob 75006 43 25 30 60 fax 40 46 83 56 St-Germain

HÔTEL MOLIÈRE
On quiet street near the Louvre and Opéra. Well-appointed, reasonably priced rooms, and helpful staff.
G5 21 rue Molière 75001 42 96 22 01 fax 42 60 48 68 Pyramides

HÔTEL LA PERLE
Renovated 17th-century building on a quiet street near St Germain. Charming breakfast patio, bar, well-appointed rooms—some with fax and Jacuzzi.
G6 14 rue des Canettes, 75006 43 29 10 10 fax 46 34 51 04 Mabillon

A moderately priced hotel will charge 500–1000F for a single room.

3-Star rating

All these three-star establishments are obvious favorites with business travelers, so it is virtually impossible to find rooms during trade-fair seasons such as May/early June and mid-September/October. In summer many offer discounts as their clientèle shrinks. All rooms are equipped with color TV, direct-dial phone, private bath or shower rooms, minibar, and most with hair dryer. Air conditioning is not general but elevators are.

Budget Accommodations

You should be able to find a single room in a budget hotel for under 500FF.

Budget hotels

Gone are the heady days when Paris was peppered with atmospheric one-star hotels with their inimitable signs *Eau à tous les étages* (water on every floor). Now there are bath or shower rooms in every bedroom, and correspondingly higher prices, and smaller rooms. So don't expect to swing cats in budget hotel rooms, but do expect breakfast and receptionists who speak a second language in every hotel with two or more stars.

GRAND HÔTEL MALHER
Recently renovated family hotel with 31 well-equipped rooms and an excellent location in the Marais.
J6 5 rue Malher 75004 42 72 60 92 fax 42 72 25 37 St-Paul

GRAND HÔTEL DE SUEZ
50-room hotel in central location on busy boulevard. Good value but lacks atmosphere.
H6 31 Boulevard St-Michel 75005 46 34 08 02 fax 40 51 79 44 Cluny la Sorbonne

HÔTEL ANDRÉ GILL
Charming courtyard setting on quiet side-street close to Pigalle. Renovated rooms, reasonably priced.
G3 4 rue André Gill 75018 42 62 48 48 fax 42 62 77 92 Pigalle

HÔTEL DU COLLÈGE DE FRANCE
Tranquil 29-roomed establishment near the Sorbonne. Some 6th-floor rooms offer glimpse of Notre-Dame.
H7 7 rue Thénard 75005 43 26 78 36 fax 46 34 58 29 Maubert-Mutualité

HÔTEL ESMERALDA
Very popular dollhouse hotel near Notre-Dame. Reasonably priced, book well ahead.
H6 4 rue St-Julien-le-Pauvre 75005 43 54 19 20 fax 40 51 00 68 St Michel

HÔTEL ISTRIA
Legendary Montparnasse hotel once frequented by Rilke, Duchamp, and Man Ray. Twenty-six atmospheric rooms and friendly staff.
G8 29 rue Campagne Première 75014 43 20 91 82 fax 43 22 48 45 Raspail

HÔTEL JARDIN DES PLANTES
Pretty hotel with good facilities overlooking botanical gardens.
H7 5 rue Linné 75005 47 07 06 20 fax 47 07 62 74 Jussieu

HÔTEL KENSINGTON
Convenient for the Eiffel Tower and Champ de Mars. An upscale address for a pleasant little hotel with fully renovated rooms.
E6 79 Avenue de la Bourdonnais 75007 47 05 74 00 fax 47 05 25 81 Ecole-Militaire

HÔTEL LINDBERGH
Modernized hotel on tranquil side-street near busy crossroads and shops of St-Germain. Well-equipped rooms and polyglot staff.
F7 5 rue Chomel 75007 45 48 35 53 fax 45 49 31 48 Sèvres-Babylone

HÔTEL LION D'OR
Small family hotel with adequately modernized rooms and very helpful staff. Good value for its central location.
G5 5 rue de la Sourdière 75001 42 60 79 04 fax 42 60 09 14 Tuileries

HÔTEL MICHELET-ODÉON
Reasonable rates and quiet location next to

Théâtre de l'Odéon. No frills, but helpful service.
G7 6 Place de l'Odéon 75006 46 34 27 80 fax 46 34 55 35 Odéon

HÔTEL DE LA PLACE DES VOSGES
Charming 17th-century town house in quiet street close to Place des Vosges. Basic comforts, excellent location.
J6 12 rue Birague 75004 42 72 60 46 fax 42 72 02 64 Bastille

HÔTEL PRIMA-LEPIC
In cleaner air up the hill of Montmartre, a bright hotel with well-decorated if smallish rooms and a courtyard-style reception area.
G3 29 rue Lepic 75018 46 06 44 64 fax 46 06 66 11 Abbesses

HÔTEL RÉCAMIER
Tranquil, friendly little hotel close to St-Germain and Luxembourg gardens.
G7 3 bis Place St-Sulpice 75006 43 26 04 89 St-Sulpice

HÔTEL DE ROUEN
Very cheap 22-room hotel with surprisingly well-equipped rooms. Central location near Louvre and Palais Royal.
G5 42 rue Croix-des-Petits-Champs 75001 42 61 38 21 Louvre

HÔTEL DU 7E ART
Cinephile's hotel decorated with movie photos and memorabilia. Great location in the Marais and reasonably priced rooms.
J6 20 rue Saint-Paul 75004 42 77 04 03 fax 42 77 69 10 St-Paul

HÔTEL SOLFÉRINO
A rare budget hotel in the chic 7th. Antique furniture. Opposite Musée d'Orsay on quiet street. Excellent value.
F6 91 rue de Lille 75007 47 05 85 54 fax 45 55 51 16 Solférino

HÔTEL DE LA SORBONNE
On quiet side street near the Sorbonne. Small but comfortable rooms.Well-established and unpretentious.
H7 6 rue Victor-Cousin 75005 43 54 58 08 fax 40 51 05 18 Cluny

HÔTEL DU VIEUX SAULE
On a quiet street north of Marais. Modernized, with reasonable facilities.
J5 6 rue de Picardie 75003 42 72 01 14 fax 40 27 88 21 Filles du Calvaire

SUPER HÔTEL
Near Père Lachaise cemetery. Good value, easy transportation, comfortable rooms.
M5 208 rue des Pyrénées 75020 46 36 97 48 fax 46 36 26 10 Gambetta

TIMHÔTEL LE LOUVRE
One of small chain with reliable amenities and reasonably priced rooms. Well situated for Louvre and Les Halles on quiet street.
G5 4 rue Croix des Petits-Champs 75001 42 60 34 86 fax 42 60 10 39 Louvre

Bed and breakfast

Bed-and-breakfast systems now exist to fix up visitors with host families. Try Bed and Breakfast 1 43 35 11 26 fax 40 47 69 20; France Lodge 42 46 68 19 fax 42 46 65 61; International Café Couette 42 94 92 00 fax 42 94 93 12; Accueil France Famille 45 54 22 39 fax 45 58 43 25. For those who want to stay longer and rent furnished accommodations, the best source is the free classified ads magazine "France-USA Contacts" (FUSAC). It is available at English bookshops and student travel agencies.

Haute Cuisine

The restaurants on the following pages are in three price categories:

$$$ over 300FF per person
$$ up to 300FF per person
$ up to 120FF per person

French mean cuisine

"The only cooks in the civilized world are French. Other races have different interpretations of food. Only the French mean *cuisine* because their qualities—rapidity, decision-making, tact—are used. Who has ever seen a foreigner succeed in making a white sauce?"
—Nestor Roqueplan (1804–70), Editor of *Le Figaro*

Rose-tinted dining

Le Pré Catalan ($$$) has an outdoor setting near the rose gardens of the Parc Bagatelle. Excellent seasonal dishes and exquisite desserts. (Bois de Boulogne, Route de Suresnes 75016, 45 24 55 58).

LE BRISTOL ($$$)
Uniquely elegant 18th-century oval-shaped restaurant, renowned for exquisite seafood and impeccable service.
E4 112 Faubourg St-Honoré 75008 42 66 91 45 Daily Miromesnil

LE GRAND VEFOUR ($$$)
Superb late-18th-century setting under arcades of Palais Royal, with ghosts of Napoleon, Colette and Sartre. Classic French cuisine. Relatively reasonably priced lunch menu.
G5 17 rue du Beaujolais 75001 42 96 56 27 Closed Sat–Sun and August Palais-Royal/Musée du Louvre

GUY SAVOY ($$$)
One of Paris's top young chefs continues to surprise with contrasting flavors and textures. Efficient service and contemporary décor.
D4 18 rue Troyon 75017 43 80 40 61 Closed Sat–Sun Charles-de-Gaulle-Etoile

JOËL ROBUCHON ($$$)
Temple of Parisian *nouvelle cuisine* in pastel-colored setting. Book and save well ahead.
C5 59 Ave Raymond Poincaré 75116 47 27 12 27 Closed Sat–Sun, Jul Trocadéro

LASSERRE ($$$)
A favorite with foreign visitors for impeccable service and cuisine. An extra is the sliding roof.
E5 17 Avenue Franklin D.-Roosevelt 75008 43 59 53 43 Closed all Sun and Mon lunch, Aug Franklin-D-Roosevelt

LUCAS-CARTON ($$$)
Majorelle's art-nouveau décor is the haunt of the dressy rich and famous. Try the roast pigeon with coriander.
F5 9 Place de la Madeleine 75008 42 65 22 90 Closed Sat–Sun, Aug, 24 Dec–3 Jan Madeleine

MICHEL ROSTANG ($$$)
Rostang still holds his own in the Parisian gastronomy stakes with interesting combinations, superb cheeses, and desserts. Elegant table settings.
D3 20 rue Rennequin 75017 47 63 40 77 Closed Sun Pereire

TAILLEVENT ($$$)
Intimate restaurant with a confirmed reputation—advance booking essential. Inventive cuisine—try the curried ravioli snails. Superlative wine list.
E4 15 rue Lamennais 75008 44 95 15 01 Closed Sat–Sun, Aug, public holidays Georges V

LA TOUR D'ARGENT ($$$)
Legendary sanctuary of *canard au sang* but lighter dishes do exist. Fabulous view over the Ile Saint-Louis, warm atmosphere, and great wine cellar.
H7 15–17 Quai de la Tournelle 75005 43 54 23 31 Closed Mon Maubert-Mutualité

REGIONAL FRENCH RESTAURANTS

AUBERGE BRESSANE ($/$$)
Delectable dishes from eastern France in a mock medieval décor. Impressive wine list of Bordeaux and Burgundies. Excellent-value lunch menus.
E6 16 Avenue de la Motte Picquet 75007 47 05 98 37 Closed Sat lunch Latour-Maubourg

LA BARACANE ($$)
Tiny, tastefully decorated restaurant whose menu homes in on Gascony and duck. Reasonably priced though limited choice in set lunch/dinner.
J6 38 rue des Tournelles 75004 42 71 43 33 Closed Sat lunch, Sun Bastille

BRASSERIE FLO ($$)
Spectacular Alsatian brasserie which dishes up mountains of delicious *choucroute spéciale*. Noisy, popular, chaotic.
H4 7 rue des Petites Ecuries 75010 47 70 13 59 Open daily until 1AM Château d'Eau

LE CAVEAU DU PALAIS ($$)
A wonderful old classic. long-time favorite with Yves Montand and Simone Signoret. Homey regional cooking.
G6 17/19 Place Dauphine 75001 43 26 04 28 Closed Sat, Sun Pont Neuf

CHEZ BENOIT ($$$)
Longstanding favorite, classic regional dishes. Booking advisable.
H5 20 rue St-Martin 75004 42 72 25 76 Open daily Rambuteau

LE CLODENIS ($$)
Intimate, discreet restaurant which serves aromatic Provençal dishes.
G2 57 rue Caulaincourt 75018 46 06 20 26 Closed Sun–Mon Lamarck-Caulaincourt

LE CROQUANT ($$)
Reworked landmarks of southwest cuisine. Sublime *confit de canard*.
C8 28 rue Jean-Maridor 75015 45 58 50 83 Closed Sun eve, Mon Lourmel

AUX FINS GOURMETS ($$)
Somewhat faded 1920s splendor serving copious portions of Basque and Béarnais cuisine.
F6 213 Boulevard St-Germain 75007 42 22 06 57 Closed Mon lunch, Sun Rue du Bac

LOUIS LANDES ($$)
Warm atmosphere, traditional dishes from the southwest. Monthly dinners round a theme, wine tastings.
F9 157 Avenue du Maine 75014 45 43 08 04 Sat lunch, Sun Mouton-Duvernet

LE SUD ($$)
Vibrant colors, plenty of foliage, and Provençal specialities such as *boeuf en daube*.
C3 91 Boulevard Gouvion-St-Cyr 75017 45 74 02 77 Closed Sun Porte Maillot

Alsace and the southwest

Gastronomically speaking, Alsace and the southwest are probably the best represented regions in Paris. Numerous brasseries churn out *choucroute* (sauerkraut), but it is the southwest that carries off the prizes with its variations on goose and duck. Recent research has found that inhabitants of this region have unexpectedly low rates of cardiac disease—despite daily consumption of cholesterol-high *foie gras*.

Asian & Italian Restaurants

13th Arrondissement

The Parisian Chinese community is concentrated in Belleville, where it coexists with Arabs and Africans, in the 3rd *arrondissement,* where invisible sweatshops churn out cheap leather goods, and above all in the 13th *arrondissement* (métros Tolbiac and Porte d'Ivry). Here Chinese New Year is celebrated with dragon parades in late-January to early February. Gastronomically speaking it offers a fantastic array of Indochinese and Chinese restaurants and soup kitchens—all at budget prices.

ASIAN

BHAI BHAI SWEETS($)
In a dilapidated covered passageway, the hub of Paris's Little India. Not as spicy-hot as it could be, but tasty curries.
H4 77 Passage Brady 75010 42 46 77 29
Open daily Strasbourg St Denis

CHEZ ROSINE ($$)
Orchestrated by charismatic Rosine Ek from Cambodia. Succulent, imaginative dishes. Sophisticated.
G5 12 rue du Mont Thabor 75001 49 27 09 23
Closed Mon lunch, Sun

CHIENG-MAI ($$)
Elegant Thai restaurant. Subtle flavors, fish steamed in banana leaf, grilled spicy mussels, and charming service.
H7 12 rue Frédéric-Sauton 75005 43 25 45 45
Closed Sun, part of Aug
Maubert-Mutualité

CHINE ELYSÉES ($)
Off Champs-Elysées, useful for pre- or post-cinema. A rare budget restaurant for the area, with Peking specialities.
E4 6 rue du Colisée 75008 43 59 83 46
Open daily Franklin-Roosevelt

HAWAÏ ($)
Huge, animated canteen-style restaurant, popular with local Chinese. Generous soups, Southeast Asian specialties.
J10 87 Avenue d'Ivry 75013 45 86 91 90
Open daily Porte d'Ivry

KAPPA ($$)
Family-style, Japanese sushi restaurant. Animated, warm atmosphere.
G6 6 rue des Ciseaux 75006 43 26 33 31
Closed Sun St-Germain-des-Prés

LAO SIAM ($)
Wide selection of Southeast Asian cuisines: jumbo shrimp sautéed in ginger and chives or a whole crab cooked in coconut milk and chilli pepper.
K4 49 rue de Belleville 75011 40 40 09 68
Open daily Belleville

LE NIOULLAVILLE ($)
Vast, kitsch Hong-Kong-style restaurant with long menu of Chinese, Laotian, Thai, and Vietnamese specialties.
K4 32-4 rue de l'Orillon 75011 43 38 95 23
Closed Sun evening
Belleville

PATTAYA ($)
Unpretentious, with outside tables in summer. Delicious shrimp and lemon-grass soup and other Thai dishes.
H5 29 rue Etienne-Marcel 75001 42 33 98 09
Open daily Les Halles

PHÖ DONG-HUONG ($)
Popular Vietnamese family "canteen" which serves generous soups, seafood, and meat dishes. Bustling atmosphere, distinct smoking and no-smoking sections.
K4 14 rue Louis Bonnet 75011 43 57 42 81
Closed Tue Belleville

TAN DINH ($$)
Upscale Vietnamese cuisine, in an elegantly designed restaurant just behind the Musée d'Orsay. Impressive wine list and polished service.
F6 60 rue de Verneuil 75007 45 44 04 84
Closed Sun Rue du Bac

YAMAMOTO ($)
Super-fresh sushi bar with excellent-value set lunches. Popular, so crowded until 2PM. Less animated in the evening.
G5 6 rue Chabanais 75002 49 27 96 26
Closed Sun Bourse

YUGARAJ ($$)
One of Paris's best Indian restaurants. Discreet, elegant atmosphere, charming Sri Lankan waiters, excellent-value "Delhi-Express" lunch menu.
G6 14 rue Dauphine 75006 43 26 44 91
Closed Mon lunch Pont Neuf

ITALIAN

CASA BINI ($$)
Chic but relaxed, a favorite with Catherine Deneuve. Carpaccio and Tuscan dishes are specialities.
G6 36 rue Grégoire de Tours 75006 46 34 05 60
Closed Sat, Sun lunch
Odéon

L'ENOTECA ($$)
Colorfully designed upscale Italian restaurant/wine-bar in the Marais. Delicious buffet of *antipasto* and refined pasta dishes.
J6 25 rue Charles V 75004 42 78 91 44
Open daily St Paul

PASTAVINO ($)
Bresaola and choice of three freshly prepared pasta dishes every day. Clean contemporary design, cheerful service.
G6 55 rue Dauphine 75006 46 33 93 83
Open daily Odéon

SIPARIO ($$)
Theatrically styled restaurant convenient for Bastille Opera house. Wide and inventive choice of pasta, seafood, and meat dishes.
K7 69 rue de Charenton 75011 43 45 70 26
Closed Sun Bastille

STRESA ($$)
Fashionable isn't the word. Local couturiers drop in here for a quick pasta, risotto, or plate of excellent *antipasto*. Run with gusto by Neapolitan identical twins. Book ahead.
E5 7 rue de Chambiges 75008 47 23 51 62
Closed Sat, Sun Alma-Marceau

AUX TROIS CANETTES ($$)
Friendly, old-fashioned establishment plastered with nostalgic views of Naples. Extensive menu of authentic Italian classics—polenta, ossobucco, sardines.
G6 18 rue des Canettes 44 07 03 02 Sat lunch, Sun Mabillon

Panini reigns

It is said that Cathérine de Médicis, the Italian wife of Henri II, invented French cuisine in the 16th century—though Gallic opinions may differ. Italian cuisine in 20th-century Paris is, not surprisingly, very much a pizza-pasta affair, and authentic dishes are rare. However, the latest in snack fashions is the toasted *panini*, oozing mozarella and tomatoes, especially popular with businessmen near the Bourse (Stock Exchange).

Arab Restaurants

Couscous and tajine

Couscous is a mound of steamed semolina which is accompanied by a tureen of freshly cooked vegetables (onion, tomato, carrot, potato, zucchini) and the meat (or not) of your choice, from grilled lamb kabobs (*brochettes*) to chicken or *merguez* (spicy sausages). *Tajine* is a delicious all-in-one stew, traditionally cooked in a covered terra-cotta dish, which may combine lamb and prunes or chicken, pickled lemon, and olives.

AL DAR ($$)
Luxurious but over air-conditioned restaurant, highly regarded by Lebanese community. Take out section.
H7 8/10 rue Frédéric Sauton 75005 43 25 17 15 Open daily Maubert-Mutualité

L'ATLAS ($$)
Fabulous kitsch juxtaposition of Louis XIII chairs, Moroccan mosaics, and genuine smiles. Diverse menu includes 12 types of *couscous*, pigeon, and other specialties
H7 12 Boulevard St-Germain 75005 46 33 86 98 Open daily Maubert-Mutualité

CAFÉ MODERNE ($)
Generous *couscous* and *tajines* as well as basic steaks and fish. 1930s décor. North African or French wines.
K6 19 rue Keller 75011 47 00 53 62 Closed Sun Bastille

LES CÈDRES DU LIBAN ($)
A Lebanese institution with reasonable prices. Friendly service, and excellent *taboulé*, hummus, and spicy meat dishes.
F7 5 Avenue du Maine 75014 42 22 35 18 Open daily Montparnasse-Bienvenue

DARKOUM ($$)
Refined Moroccan cuisine—seafood, *pastilla*, *couscous*, and *tajines*—in a spacious Arabian Nights interior.
G5 44 rue Sainte Anne 75002 42 96 83 76 Closed Sat lunch Bourse

DÎLAN ($)
Simple, unpretentious restaurant which serves wholesome Kurdish and Turkish dishes.
H5 11 rue Mandar 75002 42 21 46 38 Closed Sat & Sun lunch Les Halles

JO GOLDENBERG ($$)
Flashy kosher deli/restaurant in the heart of the Jewish quarter. *Gefilte* fish, *pickel fleisch*, *tarama*, and other specialties.
J6 7 rue des Rosiers 75004 48 87 20 16 Open daily St Paul

LE MANSOURIA ($$)
Elegant décor, aromatic *tajines* though over-crowded on Saturdays.
L7 11 rue Faidherbe 75011 43 71 00 16 Closed Mon lunch, Sun Faidherbe-Chaligny

NOURA ($$)
Upscale busy Lebanese snack bar with takeout service, brother of the plush Pavillon Noura down the road (47 20 33 33).
D4 27 Avenue Marceau 75116 47 23 02 20 Open daily Charles-de-Gaulle-Etoile

TIMGAD ($$$)
Spectacular Moorish décor. Delicate *pastilla*, perfect *couscous*, attentive service. Booking recommended.
D4 21 rue Brunel 75017 45 74 23 70 Open daily Argentine

Brasseries & Bistros

LE BALZAR ($$)
Fashionable brasserie near the Sorbonne. Seafood, pigs' trotters, *cassoulet*. Camus and Sartre had their last argument here.
H7 49 rue des Ecoles 75005 43 54 13 67
Closed Aug Cluny

BOFINGER ($$)
Claims to be Paris's oldest brasserie (1864). Soaring glass dome, mirrored interior, chandeliers and seafood, *choucroute*, and steaks.
J6 5 rue de la Bastille 75004 42 72 87 82
Open daily Bastille

BRASSERIE STELLA ($$)
Original 1950s décor in heart of chic 16th *arrondissement*. Seafood, oysters, and wines from Sancerre and Beaujolais vineyards.
C5 133 Avenue Victor-Hugo 75016 47 27 60 54
Open daily Victor Hugo

CHEZ PAUL ($$)
A mecca for Bastille art-dealers and artists, essential to book. Delicious stuffed rabbit, *steak tartare*. Mediocre service.
K6 13 rue de Charonne 75011 47 00 34 57
Open daily Ledru-Rollin

LA COUPOLE ($$)
A Montparnassian institution since the 1920s. Wide choice of brasserie food, reasonable late-night menu (after 11PM).
F7 102 Boulevard du Montparnasse 75014 43 20 14 20 Open daily Vavin

LE DROUOT ($)
Art Deco canteen belonging to famous Chartier (along the road). Far easier to find a table here and food is equally good value.
G5 103 rue de Richelieu 75002 42 96 68 23
Open daily Richelieu-Drouot

LE GRAND COLBERT ($$)
Restored 19th-century brasserie opening on to the Galerie Colbert. Good seafood and cheerful atmosphere.
G5 2 rue Vivienne 75002 42 86 87 88
Open daily Bourse

AU PETIT RICHE ($$)
Wonderful old 1880s bistro. Reliable traditional cuisine and good Loire wines.
G4 25 rue Le Peletier 75009 47 70 68 68
Closed Sun Richelieu-Drouot

LE PETIT SAINT-BENOÎT ($)
Popular old St-Germain classic with décor barely changed since the 1930s. Outside tables in summer.
G6 4 rue Saint-Benoît 75006 42 60 27 92
Closed Sat, Sun St-Germain-des-Prés

AU VIEUX CHÊNE ($)
Pleasantly aged bistro east of the Bastille. Excellent value traditional dishes, friendly service.
L7 7 rue du Dahomey 75011 43 71 67 69
Closed Sun Faidherbe-Chaligny

La Coupole

Horror struck Parisian hearts in the mid-1980s when it was announced that La Coupole had been bought by property developers and several floors were to be added on top. This happened, but the famous old murals (by Juan Gris, Soutine, Chagall, Delaunay, and many more) have been reinstated, the red velvet seats preserved and the Art Deco lights duly restored. The 1920's décor is now classified as a historic monument.

Salons de Thé

Mariage-Frères

It's hard to escape from Mariage-Frères without a minor investment in their tastefully presented products—whether a decorative can of obscure Japanese green tea, a Chinese teapot, a tea brick, or a delicately tea-scented candle. The Mariage brothers started importing tea to France back in 1854 and the choice now extends to over 400 varieties. Reading the menu is an exotic excursion through India to the Far East.

ANGÉLINA ($$)
Overpriced and overrated lunches but exquisite cakes and hot chocolate make it a favorite for tea. Proustian Belle-Epoque décor.
G5 226 rue de Rivoli 75001 42 60 82 00 Closed evenings, Aug Tuileries

LES ENFANTS GÂTÉS ($)
Deep armchairs, plants, and pictures. Good choice of teas, juices, salads, tarts, cakes. Fills up fast for weekend brunches.
J6 43 rue des Francs-Bourgeois 75004 42 77 07 63 Open daily until 7:30PM Rambuteau

LE FLORE EN L'ILE ($)
Good teas, cakes, and above all Berthillon sorbets and ice creams. Doubles as a café, open late, and throws in a free view of Notre-Dame.
H6 42 Quai d'Orléans 75004 43 29 88 27 Open daily Pont-Marie

LADURÉE ($$)
Rides on the back of an illustrious past and local luxury shoppers. Avoid overpriced lunches. Tea and cakes under a ceiling fresco of a cherubic pastry chef.
F5 18 rue Royale 75008 42 60 21 79 Closed Sun, Aug Concorde

LE LOIR DANS LA THÉIÈRE ($)
Established local favorite, salads, vegetable tarts, cakes, and plenty of tea and fruit juices.
J6 3 rue des Rosiers 75004 42 72 90 61 Open daily until 7PM St Paul

MARIAGES-FRÈRES ($$)
Chic, discreet tea shop with elegant upstairs tea room perfect for nonsmoking tête-à-têtes over tasty cakes or Sunday brunch. Sibling in the Marais at 30/32 rue du Bourg Tibourg.
42 72 28 11 G6 13 rue des Grands Augustins 75006 40 51 82 50 Open daily until 7:30PM Odéon

LA PAGODE ($)
Exotic tea room attached to extraordinary cinema housed in an ornate Chinese pagoda. Overlooks small Japanese garden.
F6 57bis rue de Babylone 75007 47 05 12 15 Afternoons daily St-François-Xavier

A PRIORI THÉ ($$)
A favorite with fashion crowd, essential to book at lunch. Light lunches, teas, American cakes.
G5 36 Galerie Vivienne 75002 42 97 48 75 Open daily until 7PM Bourse

TCH'A ($)
Sells 40 varieties of Chinese tea and serves delicious light lunches. Traditional service, aesthetic décor.
G6 6 rue du Pont de Lodi 75006 43 29 61 31 Closed Mon Pont-Neuf

MISCELLANEOUS RESTAURANTS

MA BOURGOGNE ($$)
Perfect for a summer lunch or dinner. Hearty, unpretentious food or just stop for a drink.
J6 · 19 Place des Vosges 75004 · 42 78 44 64 · Open daily, closed in Feb · Chemin Vert

CAFÉ DE L'INDUSTRIE ($)
Spacious, relaxed café-restaurant-tea room open until 1:30AM. Whiffs of 1970s, rock music, and reasonable though basic food.
K6 · 16 rue St-Sabin 75011 · 47 00 13 53 · Closed Sat · Bastille

AUX CHARPENTIERS ($$)
Solid French cuisine in a popular neighborhood restaurant dedicated to the carpenters' guild. Daily specialties.
G6 · 10 rue Mabillon 75006 · 43 26 30 05 · Open daily · Mabillon

LA GALERIE ($)
Pleasant relief from the tourist haunts of Montmartre. Very good value set lunch and dinner menus which may include salmon ravioli or duck with cherries. Cheerful and friendly.
G3 · 16 rue Tholozé 75018 · 42 59 25 76 · Closed Sun · Abbesses

JOE ALLEN ($)
Reliable hamburger-based fare served with humor and background music in a still fashionable late-night haunt of Les Halles.
H5 · 30 rue Pierre Lescot 75001 · 42 36 70 13 · Open daily · Etienne-Marcel

ORESTIAS ($)
Pushy, lively Greek restaurant. Good value, above all the giant shoulder of lamb. Highlight is the chandelier.
G6 · 4 rue Grégoire de Tours 75006 · 43 54 62 01 · Closed Sun · Odéon

LA POTÉE DES HALLES ($/$$)
Famed for its delicious *potée* (a steaming pot of stewed meat and vegetables) and other regional dishes. Exceptional Belle Epoque interior.
H5 · 3 rue Etienne-Marcel 75001 · 42 36 18 68 · Closed Sat lunch, Sun · Etienne-Marcel

PRUNIER ($$$)
Recently refurbished to return to former art-deco splendor. Glamorous clientèle indulges in excellent fresh seafood specialties under the accomplished eye of a former Taillevent director.
D4 · 16 Avenue Victor Hugo 75016 · 44 17 35 85 · Closed Sun eve, Mon · Charles-de-Gaulle-Etoile

WILLI'S WINE BAR ($$)
Cheerful, British-owned restaurant/wine bar with extensive international wine list. Fresh French cuisine plus the inimitable Cambridge dessert.
G5 · 13 rue des Petits Champs 75001 · 42 61 05 09 · Closed Sun · Palais-Royal

Pharamond

Alexandre Pharamond served his first plate of *tripes à la mode de Caen* in 1870, two doors from the site of the present restaurant. After he moved to No. 24 the restaurant was entirely redecorated for the 1900 Exposition Universelle and most of this structure and decoration has been preserved. The pretty floral and vegetal friezes which cover the walls of the rooms once adorned the entire four-floor façade. A sanctuary for lovers of tripe, pigs' trotters, and *andouillette*. Prices are high and booking essential.
H5 · 24 rue de la Grande Truanderie 75001 · 42 33 06 72 · Closed Mon lunch, Sun, Jul · Les Halles

Department Stores & Designer Boutiques

Opening hours

Parisian opening hours follow a Monday–Saturday pattern. Smaller shops generally open by 10AM, sometimes closing for lunch, and shut at 7PM. Avoid shopping on Saturdays, when every citizen seems to hit the streets, and take advantage of department store late-opening nights. Chain stores such as Prisunic and Monoprix are useful for picking up inexpensive household goods and even fashion accessories.

DEPARTMENT STORES

BHV (Bazar de l'Hôtel de Ville)

The do-it-yourself mecca. Browse among the basement nuts and bolts, choose paint or have wood cut on the 5th floor.

H6 52/64 rue de Rivoli, 75004 42 74 90 00 Mon–Sat 9:30–7, except Wed 9:30AM–10PM Hôtel-de-Ville

LE BON MARCHÉ RIVE GAUCHE

Very BCBG (*bon chic bon genre*). Gourmet food department, designer clothes, household linens, haberdashery, and excellent basement bookstore.

F7 22 rue de Sèvres 75007 44 39 80 00 Mon–Sat 9:30–7 Sèvres-Babylone

GALERIES LAFAYETTE

Under a giant glass dome, an enticing display of everything a home and its inhabitants need. Marginally better quality and pricier than Printemps. Top fashion designers are all represented and accessories are endless. Smaller branch by the Tour Montparnasse.

G4 40 Boulevard Haussmann 75009 42 82 34 56 Mon–Sat 9:30–6:45, except Thu 9:30–9 Chaussée d'Antin

PRINTEMPS

A classic for men's and women's fashion, accessories, household goods, furniture, designer gadgets, and more. Budget-conscious fashion-victims should look for the store's own collection under the label Sélection Printemps.

G4 64 Boulevard Haussmann 75009 42 82 50 00 Mon–Sat 9:35–7, except Thu 9.35AM–10PM Havre-Caumartin

SAMARITAINE

Labyrinthine department store with main store in Magasin II, a superb 1904 construction. Good basement hardware section. Fashion is so-so, but toy department is a paradise for kids. Useful separate store for sports equipment and clothes.

H6 19 rue de la Monnaie 75001 40 41 20 20 Mon–Sat 9:30–7, except Thu 9:30AM–10PM Pont-Neuf

LES TROIS QUARTIERS

Mainly fashion, perfumes, accessories, and household goods aimed at a more mature clientèle.

F5 23 Boulevard de la Madeleine 75001 42 97 80 12 Mon–Sat 10–7 Madeleine

DESIGNER BOUTIQUES

AGNÈS B

Pioneering designer who now rests on her comfortable reputation. Her shops monopolize most of this street. Still a favorite for her unchanging classics but fabrics and cut are no longer what they were.

Children's and men's clothes too.
H5 1-6 rue du Jour 75001 45 08 56 56 Les Halles

AMELIA MENDES
Interesting fabrics and cuts, young and chic label by KYO who also designs for Dior and Scherrer at much less affordable prices.
G5 8 rue de la Vrillière 75001 42 61 07 30 Bourse

BARBARA BUI
Silky flowing fabrics in subtle colors, well-cut suits, and a superbly designed boutique by Pucci de Rossi. One of Paris's most talented young designers.
H5 23 rue Etienne Marcel 75001 40 26 43 65 Etienne-Marcel

CHANTAL THOMASS
Paris's sexiest clothes shop, suspiciously reminiscent of an upscale brothel. Frills and thrills, stockings, lacey lingerie, and some equally seductive clothes.
G5 1 rue Vivienne 75001 40 15 01 36 Bourse

DOROTHÉE BIS
Classically imaginative knitwear in colorful, supple styles, popular for more mature avant-garde clientèle.
H5 46 rue Etienne-Marcel 75002 42 21 04 00 Les Halles

IRIÉ
Former assistant of Kenzo who creates superbly cut and accessibly priced separates. A pioneer on this discreet street.
G6 8 rue du Pré-aux-Clercs 75007 42 61 18 28 St-Germain-des-Prés

KASHIYAMA
Look out for the label of Martin Margiela, a rising star from Antwerp who worked for Gaultier and now designs his own version of the avant garde.
G6 147 Boulevard St-Germain 75006 46 34 11 50 St-Germain-des-Prés

LOLITA LEMPICKA
Established inventive chic, very Parisienne. Ultrafeminine details and shop design.
J6 3bis rue des Rosiers 75004 42 74 42 94 St Paul

MICHEL KLEIN
Reliably chic from season to season. Search out the Klein d'Oeil label which offers very feminine designs for smaller budgets—but not as small as that.
G6 6 rue du Pré aux Clercs 75007 47 03 93 76 St-Germain-des-Prés

ROMEO GIGLI
Venetian carnival invades an old printers' workshop. Gigli's rich velvet, taffeta, silk, and jersey designs are presented like works of art, which they are. Men's creations on mezzanine.
J6 46 rue de Sévigné 75004 48 04 57 08 St Paul

Fashion hubs

Three epicenters of women's high fashion make clothes shopping, or mere window-gazing easy. The hub of Place des Victoires (home to Kenzo, Stephane Kélian, Plein Sud, Victoire) continues along the rue Etienne-Marcel and towards Les Halles. The Marais's enticing offerings run between the rue de Sévigné, rue des Rosiers, Place des Vosges, and side streets. Saint-Germain burgeons along and off the boulevard, rue de Grenelle, and continues up the Boulevard Raspail.

Zen cuts

Issey Miyake reigns OK! His sculptural, finely pleated creations in imaginative synthetics are sold at 3 Place des Vosges 75004 (48 87 01 86) but Plantation/Issey Miyake at 17 Boulevard Raspail 75007 (45 48 12 32) is where more accessible designs are available. And if black and white is your style, head for Yohji Yamamoto at 25 rue du Louvre 75001 (42 21 42 93) for sober geometric cuts for men and women, just a few doors apart.

Markets

Food markets

Parisians shop daily for ultra-fresh produce and perfectly oozing cheeses. Circulating food markets spring up on boulevards throughout the city (the Bastille Sunday market being particularly enormous), but permanent food markets exist from the rue Poncelet (75017) to the rue Daguerre (75014) or the Left Bank intellectuals' classic on the rue de Buci (75006). All keep provincial lunch hours, so avoid 1–4PM.

CARREAU DU TEMPLE
Covered market specializing in leather goods. Bargain hard and you may pay half the price you would in a store.
J5 Rue E. Spuller 75003 Tue–Sun 9–noon Temple

MARCHÉ D'ALIGRE
Secondhand clothes, crockery and bric-a-brac huddle in the middle of a large, low-priced food-market.
K7 Place d'Aligre 75012 Tue–Sun 8–1 Ledru-Rollin

MARCHÉ DE MONTREUIL
Jeans and jackets start at the métro, but persevere across the bridge for domestic appliances, carpets, bric-à-brac, and some great secondhand. Morning choice is best.
N6 Avenue de la Porte de Montreuil 75020 Sat–Mon 7–6 Porte de Monreuil

MARCHÉ AUX OISEAUX
Caged birds whistle and chirp for new owners every Sunday. During the week (except Mon) feathered friends make way for a flower market.
H6 Place Louis Lépine 75004 None Sun 9–7 Cité

MARCHÉ AUX PUCES DE SAINT-OUEN (►44)

MARCHÉ DE LA RUE LEPIC
Another uphill struggle, but worth it. Keep going down the other side of the hill to the rue du Poteau (Jules-Joffrin) for African foods.
G3 Rue Lepic 75018 Tue–Sat 9–1, 4–7; Sun 9–1 Abbesses

MARCHÉ DE LA RUE MONTORGUEIL
The leftovers of Les Halles food market, now a marble-paved pedestrian street with atmosphere and plenty of trendy little bars and lunch places.
H5 Rue Montorgueil 75001 Tue–Sat 9–1, 4–7; Sun 9–1 Les Halles

MARCHÉ DE LA RUE MOUFFETARD
A tourist classic straggling down a winding, hilly street. Wonderful array of fruit and vegetables and plenty of aromatic cheeses and charcuterie.Good café stops *en route*.
H8 Rue Mouffetard 75005 Tue, Thu, Sat 9–1, 4–7 Monge

MARCHÉ AUX TIMBRES
Philatelists zoom in here to buy and sell their miniature treasures.
E5 Rond-Point des Champs-Elysées 75008 Thu, Sat, Sun and holidays 9–7 Franklin-D-Roosevelt

MARCHÉ DE VANVES
A favorite with young yuppies and hot on 1950s and deco styles. Secondhand furniture, bric-a-brac, paintings, prints, and some ethnic stands.
E9 Avenue Georges Lafenestre, Avenue Marc Saugnier 75014 None Sat–Sun 7–7:30 Porte de Vanves

ART & ANTIQUES

ARTCURIAL
Large store of contemporary art (prints, jewelry, sculpture, carpets) and an excellent art bookstore.
E4 9 Avenue Matignon 75008 42 99 16 16 Tue–Sat 10:30–7:15 Franklin-D-Roosevelt

CARRÉ RIVE GAUCHE
This grid of streets is home to some of Paris's top antique dealers. Archaeological pieces, Louis XIV, XV, Empire, Japanese scrolls, 19th-century bronzes, astrolabes, prints ... it's all there.
G6 Rue du Bac, Quai Voltaire, rue des Saints-Pères, rue de l'Université 75007 Tue–Sat 10:30–7 Rue du Bac

LA COUR AUX ANTIQUAIRES
Tiny group of antique shops which sell anything from icons to porcelain, candelabra to *chaise-longues*.
F5 54 rue Faubourg St-Honoré 75008 42 66 96 63 Tue–Sat Concorde

GALERIE DOCUMENTS
Original posters and etchings from period 1890–1940 by such masters as Toulouse-Lautrec and Mucha. Mail-order service.
G6 53 rue de Seine 75006 43 54 50 68 Tue–Sat 10:30–12:30, 2:30–7 Odéon

GALERIE DURAND-DESSERT
Spectacular conversion of an old Bastille mattress factory into a conceptual art mecca.
K6 28 rue de Lappe 75011 48 06 92 23 Tue–Sat 11–7 Bastille

GALERIE MONTENAY
A longstanding contemporary art gallery where young French and foreign artists are regularly exhibited.
G6 31 rue Mazarine 75006 43 54 85 30 Tue–Sat 11–1, 2:30–7 Odéon

LOUVRE DES ANTIQUAIRES
Huge, modernized complex of antique shops which sell everything from Eastern carpets to Lalique glass, jewelry, furniture, silver, porcelain, or paintings. High prices.
G5 2 Place du Palais Royal 75001 42 97 27 00 Tue–Sun 11–7 Palais-Royal

VILLAGE SAINT-PAUL
A cluster of antique and bric-a-brac shops opening onto an enclosed square. Shops continue down the streets on either side with everything from Asian textiles to glass, old furniture or clothes.
J6 Rue Saint-Paul, rue Charlemagne 75004 Thu–Mon 11–7 St-Paul

VILLAGE SUISSE
Network of upscale furniture and antique shops in this chic residential area.
D7 54 Avenue de la Motte-Piquet & 78 Avenue de Suffren 75015 43 06 69 90 Thu–Sun 10:30–7 Motte-Piquet

Galleries

Even if you cannot afford to invest in contemporary art, Paris offers a good window on the latest movements. Art traditionally centered on the Left Bank around the rue de Seine but today the more avant-garde galleries spread from around the Centre Georges Pompidou east through the Marais to the Bastille. Pick up a free gallery map at one of the galleries and follow the creative route.

Books & Records, Design & Interior, Food & Wine

Sunday openings

Sundays now have a strong consumer itch to them with the new marble-clad Carrousel du Louvre, perfect for a rainy day. Offerings include a Virgin record/bookstore, a newsagent with a wide international selection, Bodum kitchenware, Nature et Découvertes (a fashionably "ecological" toy and gadget shop), a stylish optician, and various boutiques. Entrance is from 99 rue de Rivoli or by the Carrousel arch in the Louvre.

BOOKS & RECORDS

BRENTANO'S

Well-stocked American bookstore with good travel and art sections at back. Bilingual staff. G5 37 Avenue de l'Opéra 75001 42 61 52 50 Opéra

LA CHAMBRE CLAIRE

Excellent photography bookstore with wide range of international publications. Occasional exhibitions. G7 14 rue St-Sulpice 75006 46 34 04 31 Mon–Sat Odéon

FNAC

The main branch of this firmly established cultural chain. Books, records, cameras, audio, computer accessories. Fair-price policy reigns and staff are helpful. G7 136 rue de Rennes 75006 49 54 30 00 St Sulpice

GALIGNANI

Pleasantly traditional, spacious bookstore brimming with laden tables and shelves. Large stock of English, German, and French literature and art books. Helpful staff. G5 224 rue de Rivoli 75001 42 60 76 07 Tuileries

LA HUNE

Great for late-night browsing with weekday doors open till midnight. Excellent literary bookstore with extensive art and architecture section. French and imported books. G6 170 Boulevard St-Germain 75006 45 48 35 85 St-Germain-des-Prés

LIBRAIRIE DES FEMMES

Next to the St-Germain market, a feminist bookstore with vast choice of international women writers. G7 74 rue de Seine 75006 43 29 50 75 Odéon

VIRGIN MEGASTORE

Enormous palace of records with generous opening hours. Chic café. New branch in the Carrousel du Louvre, 99 rue de Rivoli. E4 52/60 Champs-Elysées 75008 49 53 50 00 Mon–Thu 10AM–midnight, Fri–Sat 10AM–1AM, Sun noon–midnight Franklin-D-Roosevelt

DESIGN & INTERIOR

DEHILLERIN

Food-lover's paradise, brimming with copper pans, knives, *bains maries*, sieves and more, in true traditional style. Mail-order service. H5 18 rue de la Coquillière 75001 42 36 53 13 Les Halles

EN ATTENDANT LES BARBARES

Colorful hive of primitive-baroque designer objects, from resin candlesticks to funky furniture by young French designers. H5 50 rue Etienne-Marcel 75001 42 33 37 87 Sentier

ETAMINE
Vast home-interior shop with superb objects and fabrics imported from all over the world but firmly stamped with Parisian taste.
F6 63 rue du Bac 75007 42 22 03 16 Rue du Bac

SOULEIADO
Cheerful range of fabrics, table linen, and cushions in bright, sunny Provençal prints.
G6 78 rue de Seine 75006 43 54 62 25 Mabillon

FOOD & WINE

ANDROUET
Encyclopedic range of pungent French cheeses in perfectly ripened states. Cheese restaurant attached, delivery service in Paris.
F3 41 rue d'Amsterdam 75008 48 74 26 90 Liège

FAUCHON
THE gourmet's paradise —at a price. Established luxury delicatessen offering only the best in spices, exotic fruit, tea, coffee, charcuterie, pâtisseries ... and more. Snacks available on spot.
F5 26 Place de la Madeleine 75008 47 42 60 11 Madeleine

IZRAËL
Colorful souk spilling North African and Middle Eastern goodies onto sidewalk. Sacks of grains, bottles of spices, piles of African baskets.
J6 30 rue François Miron 75004 42 72 66 23 St-Paul

LEGRAND FILLES ET FILS
Fine wines and selected groceries in a shop dating from 1890. Helpful advice, wide price range but reliable quality. Occasional wine tastings.
G5 1 rue de la Banque 75002 42 60 07 12 Bourse

LA MAISON DU MIEL
Countless types of honey—chestnut, lavender, pine-tree, acacia—presented in a pretty, tiled interior dating from 1908.
F4 24 rue Vignon 75009 47 42 26 70 Madeleine

A LA MÈRE DE FAMILLE
Original 18th-century grocery shop with shelves laden with imaginatively created chocolates, sweets, jams, and unusual groceries. Friendly service.
H4 35 rue du Faubourg Montmartre 75009 47 70 83 69 Le Peletier

ROBERT LABEYRIE
Celebrated shop which specializes in products from the Landes. Goose and duck livers, *foie gras*, truffles, dried mushrooms of all types.
H5 6 rue Montmartre 75001 45 08 95 26 Les Halles

TACHON
Unpretentious old-fashioned cheese shop, renowned for its goat, sheep and cow products.
G5 38 rue de Richelieu 75001 42 96 08 66 Palais-Royal

Ethnic attractions

Gourmets suffering from a surfeit of delectable but outrageously priced French groceries should head for Paris's ethnic areas. For Indian products the Passage Brady (75010) is unbeatable, while the nearby rue d'Enghien harbors several Turkish grocery stores. Belleville offers both Arab and Chinese specialties but for a real taste of the Far East go to the 13th *arrondissement* and the Chinese supermarket, Tang Frères, at 47 Avenue d'Ivry.

Miscellaneous & Offbeat

Window-shopping

Some Parisian streets do not fit any convenient slot and so make for intriguing window-shopping. Try rue Jean-Jacques Rousseau and Passage Véro-Dodat (75001), rue Saint Roch (75001), rue Monsieur-le-Prince and parallel rue de l'Odéon (75006), rue Saint-Sulpice, rue des Francs-Bourgeois (75004), rue du Pont Louis-Philippe (75004), or rue de la Roquette (75011). And for luxury goods take a stroll along the Faubourg Saint-Honoré (75008).

ANTHONY PETO
The male answer to Marie Mercié. Inventive and wearable men's quality headgear from top hats to berets, aimed at the young and hip.
G5 12 rue Jean-Jacques Rousseau 75001 42 21 47 15 Louvre

LES ARCHIVES DE LA PRESSE
Treasure trove of old magazines, newspapers, and catalogues.
J6 51 rue des Archives 75003 42 72 63 93 Rambuteau

L'ART DU BUREAU
High-tech and designer accessories for the desk-top, tasteful stationery.
J6 47 rue des Francs Bourgeois 75004 48 87 57 97 St-Paul

AXIS
Witty contemporary objects, plates, teapots, jewelry, clocks. Another shop at the Bastille, 13 rue de Charonne.
G6 18 rue Guénégaud 75006 43 29 66 23 Odéon

CHÉRI-BIBI
Amusing and inventive women's hats at very affordable prices. Bit of a trek but worth it.
K6 82 rue de Charonne 75011 43 70 51 72 Charonne

CHRISTIAN TORTU
Anemones, amaryllis, and apple-blossom ... the ultimate bouquet from Christian Tortu's florist shops. Wrapping is in understated brown paper bound with raffia.
G6 6 Carrefour de l'Odéon 75006 43 26 02 56 Odéon

CUISINOPHILE
Tiny little shop packed with decorative old kitchen utensils, mostly in working order.
J6 28 rue du Bourg Tibourg 75004 40 29 07 32 Hôtel-de-Ville

DEBAUVE & GALLAIS
Original wood-paneled 18th-century pharmacy which developed into a chocolate shop when medicinal properties of cocoa were discovered.
G6 30 rue des Saints-Pères 75007 45 48 54 67 St-Germain

DIPTYQUE
For over 30 years this boutique has sold its own exquisite label of perfumed candles and *eaux de toilette*. Also men's ties, scarves, and superb glasses.
H7 34 Boulevard St-Germain 75005 43 26 45 27 Maubert-Mutualité

L'HABILLEUR
End of designer lines at huge discounts. Plenty of choice, with helpful sales staff.
J5 44 rue de Poitou 75003 42 72 07 13 St-Sébastien-Froissart

IKUO
Tiny little shop, a treasure chest of interesting jewelry mainly by Japanese creators. Good value.
G6 11 rue des Grands Augustins 75006 43 29 56 39 Pont-Neuf

JEAN LAPORTE
An aromatic universe of potpourris, essences, candles, and perfumes based on floral, fruity, and spicy themes.
F6 84bis rue de Grenelle 75007 45 44 61 57
Rue du Bac

JOUETS & CIE
Vast emporium of toys, games, costumes, party gear, computer games, trains, etc. An early Philippe Starck design.
H6 11 Boulevard de Sébastopol 75001 42 33 67 67 Châtelet

MARIE MERCIÉ
Compulsive creator of extravagant hats. Choose your headgear here or in her original shop near Les Halles at 56 rue Tiquetonne.
G7 23 rue St-Sulpice 75006 43 26 45 83
Mabillon

MI-PRIX
Designer numbers at a fraction of the price, including shoes by Michel Perry.
C8 27 Boulevard Victor 75015 48 28 42 48
Porte de Versailles

MOUTON À CINQ PATTES
Cut-price designer clothes packed into a crowded shop. Another shop in the Marais at 15 rue Vieille du Temple.
G6 19 rue Grégoire des Tours 75006 43 29 73 56
Odéon

NAÏLA DE MONBRISON
Gallery showing some of the most sought-after contemporary jewelry designers' work, including Marcial Berro, Tina Chow, Mattia Bonetti.
F6 6 rue de Bourgogne 75007 47 05 11 15
Varenne

PAPIER +
Wonderful emporium of quality paper in endless subtle hues. Superbly bound books, files, and bouquets of colored pencils.
J6 9 rue du Pont Louis-Philippe 75004 42 77 70 49
Pont-Marie

SCOOTER
To get that real Les Halles look, drop in here for latest accessories: ethnic, 1960s/70s revival transformed into jewelry, bags, clothes.
H5 10 rue de Turbigo 75001 45 08 89 31
Les Halles

SI TU VEUX
Charming and affordable toystore with interesting toys, games and dressing-up gear. Separate section devoted to teddy-bear related items.
G5 68 Galerie Vivienne 75002 42 60 59 97
Bourse

TATI
Originally aimed at the emptiest purses in Paris, Tati now attracts the rich and famous but is still low-cost.Women's men's, and kids' clothes, as well as household goods.
H3 2-30 Boulevard Rochechouart 75018 42 55 13 09 Barbès-Rochechouart

Chocaholics

Chocolate came to Europe via Spain from South America. Under Louis XIV it became a fashionable drink and was served three times a week at Versailles. Paris's first chocolate shop opened in 1659, Voltaire drank up to 12 cups a day, and Napoleon apparently had a *penchant* for it first thing in the morning. But the French with their consumption of a mere 12lb. per person still lag behind the Swiss, who consume an annual 22lb., and the Belgians (15lb.).

Concerts, Jazz Clubs & Nightclubs

Church concerts

Numerous classical music concerts are held in churches—try St-Eustache, St-Germain des Prés, St-Julien le Pauvre, St-Louis en l'Ile, St. Roch, and St. Séverin. Seats are reasonably priced and the quality of music is sometimes very high. In May–September free concerts are held in parks all over the city. Programs are available at the Office du Tourisme or the Hôtel de Ville, or 40 71 76 47.

Recitals

The most prestigious venue on the classical-buff's circuit, now home to the Orchestre de Paris, is the Salle Pleyel (252 rue du Faubourg Saint-Honoré, 45 61 53 00). Chopin gave his last recital here and it is the venue for many of Paris's major concerts, often with world-famous soloists, and for radio and record recordings. Another established concert hall, the Salle Gaveau, still attracts top international opera singers or pianists in spite of its shabby appearance (45 rue de la Boétie 75008, 49 53 05 07).

CONCERT VENUES

AUDITORIUM DES HALLES

Lunchtime and early-evening concerts and recitals: classical, world-music, jazz.
H5 Forum des Halles, Porte Ste-Eustache 75001 42 36 13 90 Les Halles

CITÉ DE LA MUSIQUE

Accessible Classical, jazz, world music at this new concert hall in a rather out-of-the-way location.
L2 209 Avenue Jean-Jaurès 75019 44 84 44 84 Porte de Pantin

OPÉRA BASTILLE

Long-term teething problems continue at Paris's "people's" opera house. Opera, recitals, dance, and even theater.
K6 120 rue de Lyon 75012 44 73 13 99 Bastille

OPÉRA COMIQUE

Sumptuously decorated opera house which stages light opera, dance, and sometimes theater.
G4 5 rue Favart 75002 42 60 04 99 Richelieu-Drouot

THÉÂTRE DU CHÂTELET

Varied program of opera, symphonic music, and dance. Cheap seats for lunchtime.
H6 Place du Châtelet 75001 40 28 28 40 Châtelet

THÉÂTRE DES CHAMPS-ELYSÉES

Top international orchestras play in a high-priced, stately setting.
E5 15 Avenue Montaigne 75008 49 52 50 50 Alma-Marceau

THÉÂTRE DE LA VILLE

Modern theater with adventurous program of contemporary dance, avant-garde music, theater, and early evening recitals of world music.
H6 Place du Châtelet 75004 42 74 22 77 Châtelet

JAZZ CLUBS

BILBOQUET

Strait-laced crowd with good sprinkling of tourists. Traditional jazz, pricey cocktails. Restaurant.
G6 13 rue St-Benoît 75006 45 48 81 84 St Germain-des-Prés

CAVEAU DE LA HUCHETTE

Still going strong, a smoky basement bar with dancing and live jazz from 9:30PM.
H6 5 rue de la Huchette 75005 43 26 65 05 St Michel

CHAPELLE DES LOMBARDS

Funky Bastille haunt with hot atmosphere and live raï (Algerian rock), rap, open until dawn.
K6 19 rue de Lappe 75011 43 57 24 24 Closed Sun Bastille

NEW MORNING

One of Paris's top jazz/blues/soul bars. Good atmosphere, dedicated crowd, quality

assured. Top names require booking.
H4 7/9 rue des Petites Ecuries 75010 45 23 56 39 Château d'Eau

PASSAGE DU NORD-OUEST
Interesting experimental venue which combines jazz/rock/world music concerts with offbeat movie program. Live music Thu–Sun.
H4 13 rue du Faubourg Montmartre 75010 36 68 03 32 Rue Montmartre

LE SUNSET
Part of the Les Halles cluster, a restaurant-bar with good jazz concerts from 10PM until the small hours. Reasonably priced food.
H6 60 rue des Lombards 75001 40 26 46 60 Châtelet

LA VILLA
Top jazz names. Sleekly designed cocktail-bar setting in stylish post-modern hotel basement, open late. Book.
G6 29 rue Jacon 75006 43 26 60 00 Closed Sun St-Germain-des-Prés

NIGHTCLUBS

L'ARC
Fairly upscale club with selective door-policy. Piano-bar restaurant and interior garden.
D4 12 rue de Presbourg, 75016 45 00 45 00 From 11:30PM nightly Charles-de-Gaulle-Etoile

LES BAINS
Still number one for fashion and showbiz set. Heavy door-policing, restaurant. Go very late.
H5 7 rue du Bourg-l'Abbé 75003 48 87 01 80 Nightly Etienne-Marcel

LE BALAJO
Over 60 years old, ritzy 1930s décor, music mainly disco, techno, funk.
K6 9 rue de Lappe 75011 47 00 07 87 Thu–Sat Bastille

LE BATACLAN
An old favorite now rejuvenated. Fashion-media set with fancy dress on Fridays, mainly house music on Saturday.
K5 50 Boulevard Voltaire 75011 47 00 30 12, 47 00 55 22 Thu–Sat from 11PM Oberkampf

PIGALL'S
Latest Pigalle haunt which thunders soul, acid-jazz. Transvestites add to the funkiness.
G3 77 rue Pigalle 75009 46 27 82 82 Fri–Sat from 12PM Pigalle

RÉGINE
Flashy mature crowd, rich in media stars. Careful grooming at door so look neat—you may be lucky.
E4 49–51 rue de Ponthieu, 75008 43 59 21 13 Franklin-D-Roosevelt

LE TANGO
Unpretentious club with hot-blooded Afro-Latino rhythms, tango, salsa, reggae, and soul.
J5 13 rue au Maire 75003 42 72 17 78 Fri–Sat from 11PM Arts et-Métiers

Clubs and raves

Paris clubbing is both serious and fickle—serious because no truly cool Parisian turns up before midnight, and fickle because mass loyalties change rapidly. Most clubs keep going through the night till dawn and nearly all charge an entry on Friday and Saturday nights which usually includes a drink. For impromptu raves, theme nights, and house parties outside Paris with shuttles provided, check Pariscope's English section or key in to Minitel 3615 Party News.

Bars & Special Cinemas

BARS

BAR DU MARCHÉ
Hip watering hole with good sounds and cheerful service. Nice terrace in summer.
G6 75 rue de Seine 75006 43 26 55 15
Daily 8AM–1AM Odéon

BAR ROMAIN
Original 1905 décor brightens this bar-restaurant. Choice of over 200 cocktails, popular with more mature showbiz crowd.
G4 6 rue Caumartin 75009 47 42 98 04
Mon–Sat 12PM–2AM
Havre-Caumartin

BIRDLAND
An old St-Germain favorite. Relaxed, with great jazz records.
G6 8 rue Princesse 75006 43 26 97 59
Nightly 7PM–6AM
Mabillon

LES BOUCHONS
Late-night basement bar with occasional live jazz. Cheerful restaurant upstairs.
H6 19 rue des Halles 75001 42 33 28 73
Nightly 11:30PM until dawn
Châtelet

CAFÉ NOIR
Popular, packed late-night haunt on fringe of Les Halles. High-decibel rock and unmistakable technicolor exterior.
H5 65 rue Montmartre 75002 40 39 07 36
Daily 7:30AM–2AM, closed Sun Sentier

CAFÉ DE LA PLAGE
Bastille bohemia homes in to this small bar to tank up. Mixed crowd, regular soul/jazz concerts downstairs.
K6 59 rue de Charonne 75011 47 00 91 60
6PM–2AM; Sun, Mon 10PM–2AM Ledru-Rollin

LA CASBAH
Moorish-styled bar with dancing, fancily dressed bar staff, great cocktails and décor but supremely unfriendly bouncers.
K7 18 rue de la Forge-Royale 75011 43 71 71 89
Tue–Sat 11:30PM onwards
Faidherbe-Chaligny

CHINA CLUB
Shady red-lacquered bar/restaurant peopled by Mao-style waiters. Hip and crowded, avoid the food, go for a drink. Another bar upstairs.
K7 50 rue de Charenton 75012 43 43 82 02
Nightly 7PM–2AM Ledru-Rollin

HARRY'S BAR
Old pub atmosphere. Rowdy, mature, well-tanked up crowd.
G5 5 rue Daunou 75002 42 61 71 14 Nightly 10:30PM–4am Opéra

JACQUES MÉLAC
Inexpensive French wines by the glass or bottled for you from the barrel.
L6 42 rue Léon Frot 75011 43 70 59 27
Closed Sat–Sun, mid-Jul–mid-Aug Charonne

LILI LA TIGRESSE
Weekend cover charge at this hip hot spot in Pigalle. Ornate decor, dancing, and occasional

Cinephile's paradise
Though French film production dropped below the 100 mark in 1994 the capital is still a cinephile's paradise. With some 350 films shown each day, the choice can be tantalizing. Foreign films shown in their original languages have "VO" (*version originale*) after the title. New films come out on Wednesdays, which is also the day for all-round reductions. Gaumont and UGC offer multiple-entry cards which can be used for up to three people and save extra precious francs.

theme nights.
G3 98 rue Blanche 75009 48 74 08 25
Nightly 10PM–2AM
Blanche

MAYFLOWER
Lively, reasonably priced bar-pub that has attracted student nighthawks for years.
H7 49 rue Descartes, 75005 43 54 56 47
Daily 7AM–2AM Cardinal-Lemoine

LE MOLOKO
Cavernous popular bar on two floors. Loud rock still lets you talk.
G3 26 rue Fontaine, 75009 48 74 50 26
Daily 9:30PM–6AM
Blanche

LA TARTINE
An old daytime classic. French wines by the glass, cold platters of charcuterie and cheese.
J6 24 rue de Rivoli 75004 42 72 76 85
8:30AM–10PM, closed Tue and Aug Hôtel-de-Ville

LE TRAIN BLEU
Striking Belle-Epoque setting which functions as restaurant-bar. Food pricey; stick to drinks.
K7 1st floor, Gare de Lyon, 75012 43 43 09 06
Daily 9AM–11PM Gare de Lyon

SPECIAL CINEMAS

VIDÉOTHÈQUE DE PARIS
Movies or documentaries shot in or connected with Paris, or a changing daily program of wide-ranging film classics. Cheap day pass covers four different films.
H5 Forum des Halles, Porte Ste-Eustache 75001
40 26 34 30 Les Halles

LA CINÉMATHÈQUE FRANÇAISE
Cinema classics with foreign films always in original language.
D5 7 Avenue Albert de Mun 75016 47 04 24 24
Trocadéro

LE DOME IMAX
The world's largest hemispherical screen (12,314 square feet). Digital sound system.
Off A2 1 Place du Dôme 92905 Paris La Défense 46 92 45 45 La Défense

L'ENTREPOT
Stimulating program of French and foreign films and festivals devoted to one director. Bookstore, pleasant café.
F8 7–9 rue Francis de Pressensé 75014 45 43 41 63 Pernety

LA PAGODE
A unique cinema hall housed inside an exotic Japanese pagoda. Adjoining tea room (➤72) and garden.
F6 57 bis, rue de Babylone 75007 45 55 48 48 St-François Xavier

SALLE GARANCE
Films arranged by theme or by country. Comfortable, cheap seats. Art films connected with major exhibitions on 5th floor.
H5 Centre Georges Pompidou, rue Beaubourg 75004
42 78 37 29 Rambuteau

Steam baths

If nocturnal bar-crawling has been too much, why not sweat it out at a steambath? The hammam at the Mosquée (➤52) offers a lovely tiled interior *à la* Marrakesh and is open for men on Friday and Sunday, for women Monday, Wednesday, Thursday, Saturday. A new though pricier alternative is Les Bains du Marais, 31 rue des Blancs-Manteaux, 75004 (44 61 02 02): women, Monday–Wednesday; men Thursday, Saturday.

SPORTS

Pools and horses

Paris's municipal swimming pools have complicated opening hours which are almost entirely geared to schoolchildren. Phone beforehand to check for public hours and avoid Wednesdays and Saturdays, both favorites with children off school. Gymnase Clubs are generally open till 9PM but close on Sundays. If horse-racing is your passion, don't miss the harness racing at Vincennes with its brilliant flashes of color-coordinated horses and jockeys. Check *Paris-Turf* for race programs.

AQUABOULEVARD
Huge family complex with water-shoots, palm trees, Jacuzzis. Gym, putting greens, tennis and squash courts too—at a price.
C8 4-6 rue Louis Armand 75015 40 60 10 00 Porte de Versailles

GYMNASE CLUB
Best-equipped gymnasium in this chain. Call for details on other gyms throughout Paris. Day passes, book of 10 passes, or annual subscription.
D3 17 rue du Débarcadère 75017 45 74 14 04 Porte-Maillot

HIPPODROME D'AUTEUIL
Flat-racing and hurdles. Hosts the prestigious Prix du Président de la République hurdle race.
A6 Bois de Boulogne, 75016 42 24 47 04 Closed Jul–Aug Porte d'Auteuil

HIPPODROME DE LONGCHAMP
Longchamp is where the hats and champagne come out for the annual Prix de l'Arc de Triomphe. Regular flat-races.
A6 Bois de Boulogne 75016 42 24 13 29 Closed Jul–Aug Porte d'Auteuil, then shuttle.

HIPPODROME DE VINCENNES
Colorful harness racing pulls in the crowds. Watch out for the Prix d'Amérique, the top harness race of the season.
Vincennes 75012 49 77 17 17 Closed Jul–Aug Château de Vincennes, then shuttle

PARC DES PRINCES
Huge municipal stadium takes 50,000 spectators for major soccer and rugby games.
A8 24 rue du Commandant-Guilbaud 75016 42 88 02 76 Porte de Saint-Cloud

PISCINE DES HALLES (SUZANNE BERLIOUX)
Underground 50m pool overlooked by lush tropical garden.
H5 10 Place de la Rotonde 75001 42 36 98 44 Les Halles

PISCINE JEAN TARIS
Two 25m pools with view of Panthéon. Electronically cleaned water, so no chlorine.
H7 16 rue Thouin 75005 43 25 54 03 Cardinal-Lemoine

PISCINE QUARTIER LATIN
A 33m pool with a distinct 1930's air. Solarium, squash courts, gym, and sauna.
H7 19 rue de Pontoise 75005 43 25 31 99 Maubert-Mutualité

ROLAND-GARROS
Clay-court home to the French Tennis Open. Tickets are sold months ahead but plenty of racketeers sell seats on the day at the main entrance.
A7 2 Avenue Gordon-Bennett 75016 47 43 00 47 Porte d'Auteuil then walk or bus 32, 52, 123.

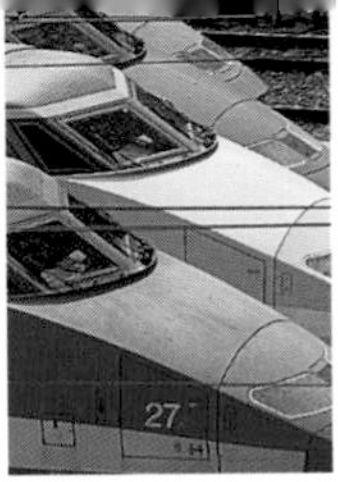

PARIS
travel facts

Arriving & Departing

Before you go

- Visas are not required for EU nationals, US, or Canadian citizens, but are obligatory for Australians and New Zealanders.
- Anyone entering France must have a valid passport (or official identity card for EU nationals).
- There are no vaccination requirements.

When to go

- "Paris in the spring" rarely starts before mid-May; June is always a glorious month.
- July and August see the Great Parisian Exodus. Cultural activities move into bottom gear, but lodging is easier.
- Avoid mid-September to mid-October, the peak trade-fair period, when hotels are full.
- Winter temperatures rarely drop below freezing but rain is common in January and March.

Arriving by train

- The Eurostar train service from London arrives at Gare du Nord.
- Trains arrive at the Gare de l'Est from Germany, Austria, and Eastern Europe.
- The Gare de Lyon serves southeast France and Italy, the Gare d'Austerlitz southwest France, Spain, and Portugal.
- The central TGV stations are Gare Montparnasse and Gare de Lyon.
- All stations have métro, bus, and taxi services.
- Ticket reservations and information for SNCF stations ☎ 45 82 50 50 (7AM–9PM daily).

Arriving by air

- Air passengers arrive either at Roissy-Charles de Gaulle airport (14 miles north of Paris) or at Orly (9 miles to the south).
- Taxis charge a surcharge at airports and at stations and also for each item of luggage carried.

Roissy

- Connections to downtown are: via a direct RER train into Châtelet-Les Halles; the Air France bus which stops at Etoile (Arc de Triomphe) and Porte Maillot; the cheaper Roissybus which terminates at rue Scribe, Opéra.
- Air France bus and Roissybus run every 15/20 minutes, 5.40AM–11PM.
- Taxis are expensive.
- Passenger information ☎ 48 62 22 80.

Orly

- Connections to downtown are via the Air France bus, which goes to Invalides every 12 minutes and stops at Porte d'Orléans, or the more economical Orlybus, which goes to Denfert-Rochereau every 15 minutes.
- Avoid Orlyrail as this involves a shuttle bus.
- Passenger information ☎ 49 75 15 15.

Customs regulations

- There are no restrictions on goods brought into France by EU citizens.
- For non-EU nationals the limits are: 200 cigarettes or 100 cigarillos or 50 cigars or 250g of tobacco, 2 litres of wine, 1 liter of spirits, 50g of perfume, 500g of coffee, and 100g of tea.
- Prescribed medicines and up to 50,000FF of currency may be imported.

Departing

- Airport tax for departing passengers is included in the price of your ticket.
- There are numerous duty-free shops at Orly and Roissy airports but not on Eurostar or other international trains.
- Allow one hour to reach Roissy airport, by any transport means, and 45 minutes for Orly.

Essential Facts

Travel insurance

- Insurance to cover theft, illness and repatriation is strongly advised.

Opening hours

- Banks: 9–4:30, Mon–Fri. Closed on public holidays and often the afternoon before.
- Post offices: 8–7, Mon–Fri; 8–noon, Sat. The Central Post Office ✉ 52 rue du Louvre, 75001 ☎ 40 28 20 00 provides a 24-hour service for post, telegrams, phone.
- Shops: 9–7 or 9:30–6:30, Mon–Sat with minor variations (smaller shops close at lunch). Arab-owned groceries stay open until 9 or 10PM, including Sun.
- Museums: National museums close on Tuesday, municipal museums on Monday. Individual opening hours vary considerably; always phone to check hours for national holidays.

National holidays

- January 1, May 1 , May 8 , Ascension (last Thursday in May), Whit Monday (early June), July 14, August 15, November 1, November 11, December 25.
- Sunday services for public transportation operate; many restaurants, large shops, and local groceries disregard national holidays.

Money matters

- The French currency is the franc (FF): 1FF = 100 centimes.

Foreign exchange

- Only banks with *change* signs change foreign currency/traveler's checks: a passport is necessary. *Bureaux de change* are open longer hours but rates can be poorer.
- Airport and station exchange desks are open 6:30AM–11PM.
- For late-night exchange in central Paris use the Exchange Corporation ✉ 63 Ave des Champs Elysées 75008 ☎ 42 56 11 35 Ⓜ Franklin-D-Roosevelt 🕑 8AM–12 noon daily.

Credit cards

- Credit cards are widely accepted.
- VISA cards (including MasterCard and Diners Club) can be used in cash dispensers. Most machines flash up instructions in the language you choose.
- American Express is less common so Amex cardholders needing cash should use American Express, ✉ 11 rue Scribe 75009 ☎ 47 14 50 00 Ⓜ Opéra.

Etiquette

- Shake hands on introduction and on leaving; once you know people better replace this with a peck on both cheeks.
- Always use *vous* unless the other person breaks into *tu*.
- It is polite to add Monsieur, Madame, or Mademoiselle when addressing strangers or salespeople.

- Always say hello and goodbye in shops.
- When calling waiters, use *Monsieur* or *Madame* (NOT *garçon*!)
- More emphasis is put on grooming than in other countries, so avoid looking messy.

Women travelers

- Women are safe to travel alone or together in Paris. Any unwanted attention should be dealt with firmly and politely.

Places of worship

- The International Center for Religious Information ✉ 6 Place du Parvis Notre-Dame, 75004 ☎ 46 33 01 01 Ⓜ St-Michel, an English-speaking service, supplies information on services and churches for Catholic, Protestant, and Orthodox worshippers.
- Protestant churches: American Church ✉ 65 Quai d'Orsay 75007 ☎ 47 05 07 99 Ⓜ Invalides. St George's English Church ✉ 7 rue Auguste Vacquerie 75016 ☎ 47 20 22 51 Ⓜ Etoile.
- Jewish: Synagogue ✉ 10 rue Pavée 75004 ☎ 42 77 81 51 Ⓜ St-Paul.
- Russian Orthodox: Saint Alexandre de la Néva ✉ 12 rue Daru 75008 ☎ 42 27 37 34 Ⓜ Courcelles.

Student travelers

- An International Student Identity Card reduces cinema charges, entrance to museums, and air and rail travel.
- AJF (Accueil des Jeunes en France) ✉ 119 rue St-Martin 75004 ☎ 42 77 87 80 Ⓜ Châtelet 🕓 9–6.30, Mon–Sat. Advice on hostel accommodations, discounts on train tickets.
- CIDJ (Centre d'Information et de Documentation Jeunesse) ✉ 101 Quai Branly 75015 ☎ 44 49 12 00 Ⓜ Bir-Hakeim 🕓 10–6, Mon–Fri. Youth information centre for jobs, courses, sports etc.

Time differences

- France is six hours ahead of New York. Clocks change at the autumn and spring solstice.

Toilets

- Cream-color public toilet booths, generally well maintained, are common.
- Every café has a toilet, although standards vary (you should not use a cafe's toilet without ordering at least a drink). Museum and restaurant WCs are generally better.

Electricity

- Voltage is 220V and sockets take two round pins.

Tourist Information Office

- Office de Tourisme de Paris ✉ 129 Avenue des Champs Elysees, 75008 ☎ 49 52 53 54 Charles-de-Gaulle Etoile. Masses of tourist information and helpful polyglot staff.

PUBLIC TRANSPORTATION

Métro

- Métro lines are identified by their terminus (*direction*) and a number; connections are indicated with orange panels marked *correspondances* on the platform.
- Blue *sortie* signs show the exits.
- First métros run at 5:30AM, last around 12:30AM.

- Keep your ticket until you exit—it has to be re-slotted on the RER and ticket inspectors prowl the métro.
- Avoid rush hours 8–9:30AM and 4:30–7PM.

Bus
- Buses should be hailed from bus stops.
- Enter, and punch your ticket into the machine beside the driver or flash your pass.
- Night buses run hourly 1:30AM–5:30PM from Place du Châtelet out to the portes and suburbs.

Maps
- Free métro/bus/RER maps are available at every station and on some buses.
- RATP information (in French) ☎ 43 46 14 14 ⌚ 6AM–9PM.
- RATP tourist office ✉ 53bis Quai des Grands Augustins 75006 ☎ 40 46 42 17.

Ticket types
- Tickets and passes function for métro, bus and RER.
- Pass prices and the number of tickets required for a ride depend on how many of five travel zones you intend to pass through.
- A *carnet* of ten tickets is considerably cheaper than individual tickets.
- *Formule 1* is a one-day pass, valid on métro, buses, and RER.
- A *Paris Visite* card gives unlimited travel for three or five days plus discounts at certain monuments.
- The *carte hebdomadaire* pass (photo required), is valid Mon–Sun.
- Monthly passes (*carte orange*), also needing a photo, are valid for one calendar month.

Taxis
- Taxis can be hailed in the street if the roof sign is illuminated or found at a rank.
- Sunday and night rates (7PM–7AM) rise considerably and extra charges are made at stations, Air France terminals, for luggage and for animals.
- Taxi drivers expect tips of 10 percent.
  Radio-taxi firms: Taxis Bleus (☎ 49 36 10 10); Alpha (☎ 45 85 85 85); G7 (☎ 47 39 47 39); Artaxi (☎ 42 41 50 50).

Media & Communications

Telephones
- Most Parisian phone booths use France Telecom phone cards (*télécarte* for 50 or 120 units), available from post offices, *tabacs*, stations, or at main métro stations. A few phone booths still use coins, particularly those in cafés.
- Cheap periods for international calls vary: for the USA and Canada 2AM–12PM daily, with lesser reductions 8PM–2AM; for Europe, Australia and New Zealand 9:30PM–8AM daily, and all day Sun;
- Repairs: 13
- Information: 12
- International information: 00 33 12 + country prefix
- In spring 1996 French telephone numbers change to 10 digits.
  19+ for international calls becomes 00+
  16+ formerly used for calling the French provinces is replaced by: 02 Northwest, 03 Northeast, 04 Southeast, 05 Southwest. All numbers in the Ile-de-France, including Paris, start with 01.

Post offices

- Stamps can be bought at *tabacs* and mail posted in any yellow postbox.
- All post offices have free access to the Minitel directory service, express courier post (Chronopost), phone booths, and photocopying machines.

Press

- The main dailies are *Le Monde* (out at 2PM), *Libération*, and *Le Figaro*.
- Weekly news magazines range from the left-wing *Le Nouvel Observateur, L'Express* (center) and *Le Point* (center-right) to *Paris Match* and *Canard Enchaîné*. For weekly listings of cultural events, buy a copy of *Pariscope* (with an English section) or *L'Officiel des Spectacles*.
- Central newspaper kiosks and newsagents stock European dailies.
- The NMPP's central bookstore (✉ 93 rue Montmartre 75002) has a comprehensive range of French and foreign press and the newsagent in the Carrousel beneath the Louvre carries American press and international fashion publications.

Radio and television

- FM stations run the gamut from current affairs on France Inter (87.8 MHz) to unadulterated rap/rock/house music on Radio Nova (101.5 MHz).
- France 2 and France 3, the state TV channels, occasionally have good documentaries and current events programs. TF1 has lightweight entertainment, and M6 is still evolving. Arte (on Channel 5), a serious Franco-German cultural channel, offers good European coverage.

EMERGENCIES

Precautions

- Watch wallets and handbags as pickpockets are active, particularly in crowded bars, flea markets, and cinemas.
- Keep traveler's check numbers separate from the checks themselves.
- Make a declaration at a local *commissariat* (police station) to claim any losses from your insurance.

Lost property

- The police lost-property office is ✉ 36 rue des Morillons 75015 🕐 8:30AM–5PM Ⓜ Convention. No phone inquiries.

Medicines and medical treatment

- Minor ailments can often be treated at pharmacies (identified by a green cross) where staff will also advise on local doctors.
- All public hospitals have a 24-hour emergency service (*urgences*) as well as specialist doctors. Payment is made on the spot but if you are hospitalized ask to see the *assistante sociale* to arrange payment directly through your insurance.
- House calls are made with SOS Médecins ☎ 47 07 77 77 or for dental problems SOS Dentistes ☎ 43 37 51 00.
- 24-hour pharmacy: Dhéry ✉ 84 Ave des Champs Elysées 75008 ☎ 45 62 02 41.
- The Drug-store chain at St-Germain, Opéra, and Champs-Elysées offers pharmacies, newsagents, cafés, and tobacconists open until 2AM.

Emergency phone numbers

- Crisis-line in English SOS Help

☎ 47 23 80 80 ⏲ 3–11PM.

- Fire (*sapeurs pompiers*) 18.
- 24-hour ambulance service (SAMU) 15.
- Police 17.
- Anti-poison ☎ 40 37 04 04.

Embassies and consulates

- US Embassy ✉ 2 Avenue Gabriel 75008 ☎ 42 96 12 02.
- US Consulate ✉ 2 rue St-Florentin 75001 ☎ 42 96 14 88.
- Canadian Embassy ✉ 35 Avenue Montaigne 75008 ☎ 44 33 29 00.
- Candadian Consulate ✉ 37 Avenue Montaigne 75008 ☎ 44 43 29 16.
- British Embassy ✉ 35 rue du Faubourg St-Honoré 75008 ☎ 42 66 91 42.
- British Consulate ✉ 9 Avenue Hoche 75008 ☎ 42 66 38 10.
- Australian Embassy ✉ 4 rue Jean Rey 75015 ☎ 40 59 33 00.
- New Zealand Embassy ✉ 7 ter rue Léonard de Vinci 75016 ☎ 45 00 24 11.

LANGUAGE

1	un	**16**	seize
2	deux	**17**	dix-sept
3	trois	**18**	dix-huit
4	quatre	**19**	dix-neuf
5	cinq	**20**	vingt
6	six	**21**	vingt-et-un
7	sept	**30**	trente
8	huit	**40**	quarante
9	neuf	**50**	cinquante
10	dix	**60**	soixante
11	onze	**70**	soixante-dix
12	douze	**80**	quatre-vingt
13	treize	**90**	quatre-vingt-dix
14	quatorze	**100**	cent
15	quinze	**1000**	mille

Preliminaries

yes/no oui/ non
please s'il vous plaît
thank you merci
excuse me excusez-moi
hello bonjour
good evening bon soir
goodbye au revoir
how are you? comment allez-vous? ça va?
very well thanks trés bien merci
how much? combien?
do you speak English? parlez-vous anglais?
I don't understand je ne comprends pas
there are 2/3 of us nous sommes deux/trois

Directions

where is/are ...? où est/sont ...?
the nearest metro le métro le plus proche
the telephone le téléphone
the bank la banque
the toilet les toilettes
the ticket office le guichet
the entrance l'entrée
the exit la sortie
here/there ici/là
turn left/right tournez à gauche/droite
straight on tout droit
behind/in front derrière/devant
in the basement au sous-sol
on the second floor au premier étage

Time

when? quand?
today aujourd'hui
yesterday hier
tomorrow demain
next week la semaine prochaine
this morning ce matin
this afternoon cet après-midi
this evening ce soir
how long? combien de temps?
three days trois jours
at what time? à quelle heure?
at 9:30AM à neuf heures et demie
at 8PM à vingt heures
at midnight à minuit
what time do you open/close?

à quelle heure ouvrez/ fermez-vous?

Hotel

reduced rate for children tarif réduit pour enfants
a single room une chambre simple
a double room une chambre double
double bed un lit matrimonial
an extra bed un lit supplementaire
with/without bathroom avec/sans salle de bains
shower douche
with phone avec téléphone
do you have ...? avez-vous ...?
a cheaper room une chambre moins chère
a bigger/quieter room une chambre plus grande/plus tranquille
pillow un oreiller
towel une serviette
soap du savon
iron un fer à repasser
hairdryer un seche cheveux
razor un rasoir

Restaurant

breakfast le petit déjeuner
lunch le déjeuner
dinner le dîner
a table for two une table pour deux
(no-)smoking area la salle (non-)fumeur
fixed-price menu le menu
the menu please la carte s'il vous plaît
salt/pepper sel/poivre
ashtray un cendrier
a carafe of water une carafe d'eau
black coffee un café
coffee with milk un café crème/café au lait
tea (with milk/lemon) un thé (au lait/citron)
some ice des glaçons
mineral water (fizzy) (de l'eau minerale (gazeuse)
a fresh orange juice une orange pressée
a whisky un scotch
draft beer une pression/un demi
a glass of white/red wine un verre de vin blanc/rouge
the check please l'addition s'il vous plaît

Shopping

how much is this? c'est combien?
do you take credit cards? acceptez-vous des cartes de credit?
where is there a cash dispenser? ou se trouve un distributeur de billets?
do you have... ? avez-vous ...
a larger size? une taille plus grande?
a smaller size? une taille plus petite?
another color? une couleur différente?
American newspapers? des jounaux américains?
it's cheap/expensive c'est pas cher/cher
a loaf of bread please une baguette s'il vous plait
a (half) kilo of... un (demi) kilo de ...
that's enough, thanks ça suffit, merci

Emergencies

I need a doctor/dentist j'ai besoin d'un médecin/dentiste
can you help me? pouvez-vous m'aider?
where is the hospital? où est l'hôpital?
where is the police station? où est le commissariat?
my passport/money has been stolen on a volé mon passeport/mon argent
I need to declare a theft j'ai besoin de faire une déclaration de vol
I've missed my flight j'ai raté mon vol
I've lost my ticket j'ai perdu mon billet
we must leave immediately nous devons partir immédiatement

INDEX

ACKNOWLEDGMENTS

The Automobile Association would like to thank the following photographers, picture libraries and associations for their assistance in the preparation of this book: F DUNLOP 44b, 45; THE LOUVRE 35b; MUSÉE CARNAVALET 46a; MUSÉE DES ARTS DÉCORATIFS 34; MUSÉE MARMOTTAN 24; REX FEATURES LTD 9

All remaining pictures are held in the Association's own library (AA PHOTO LIBRARY), with contributions from: M ADLEMAN 87a; P ENTICKNAP 18, 26b; R MOORE 21; D NOBLE 20; K PATERSON 2, 5a, 5b, 6, 25a, 25b, 28a, 28b, 30, 39a, 40, 43a, 52, 53, 56, 60; B RIEGER 1, 17, 23a, 32, 44a, 55, 57, 58, 61b; A SOUTER 7, 13a, 16, 26a, 27, 29, 31a, 31b, 41b, 43b, 48, 49a, 50, 51, 54; W VOYSEY 13b, 23b, 33a, 35a, 36a, 36b, 41a, 42, 46b, 47, 49b, 59, 61a, 87b.

Copy-editor: ***Susie Whimster***
Verifier: ***Giselle Thain***
Indexer: ***Marie Lorimer***
Original design: ***Design FX***
The author would like to thank Dominique Benedittini, Christophe Boicos and Andrew Hartley for their help during the preparation of this book.